MAJESTIC COV

MAJESTIC COV

ONCE THE KINGS OF ENGLISH RUGBY

STEVE "SCRIBBLE" EVANS

With contributions by:

Simon Maisey, Alan Joseph, John Butler,
John Lamb, John Wilkinson, Michael Austin,
Brendan Gallagher, Darrell Giles

This edition published 2021 by:

Takahe Publishing Ltd.

Registered Office:

77 Earlsdon Street, Coventry CV5 6EL

ISBN 978-1-908837-21-9

TAKAHE PUBLISHING LTD.

2021

This book, a labour of love, is dedicated to the memory of Cov legends Harry Walker, Alf Wyman, Phil Judd, Ivor Preece, Peter Jackson, Jim Broderick, John Barton and others and, on a personal note, to my late brother, David James Evans, Queen's Gallantry Medal (Royal Regiment of Fusiliers and the SAS).

Introductory Note from Simon Maisey

We call ourselves *The Three Mucky Ears* and we all love Cov for different reasons.

The author, Scribble (Steve Evans), had his happiest times reporting on Cov during his 36 years at the *Coventry Evening Telegraph*. He was named Britain's Provincial Sports Writer of the Year in 1983.

Alan Joseph has been a loyal supporter for over 50 years, following Cov both at home and away and now he runs the former players' social media.

I am a former player, who organises the former players' Cowshed Lunches and wants to see Cov back in its rightful position as the best rugby club in the country.

All the proceeds from the sale of the book are going to help Cov and the rumour that they are to keep Scribble in beer and fags is just not true!

Simon Maisey

Contents

1   Harry Walker: Mother Hen with an Equine Cavity   1

2   Alf Wyman: Cov's Father Figure   5

3   No Hiding Place for the Pimpernel   9

4   Voyage of the Last Sea Lions with a Cov Legend aboard Ship   13

5   Seven Glorious Years during the Reign of King Cole   17

6   Bottoms up … or Southern points Northwards   23

7   Boom! Evans above, It's Bomber   27

8   Wing Wizard Centurions   33

9   Dai for Coventry, England and the British Lions   39

10 Twing & Twang – The Dynamic Coventry Duo   45

11 A Bunch of Red Roses for Rosie   51

12 The Preacher Who Knocked a Wheel off the Welsh Wagon   57

13 Muncher and Cruncher – Two Iconic All-Rounders   63

14 A Presidential Salute to Coventry and England's John Barton   69

15 Billy & 'Basil', Creed & Cowman: Coventry and England
    Thoroughbreds   75

16 Let's Get Ready to … Basher!   83

17 Good Godber! What a No 8   89

18 Steve Thomas: Schoolboy Captain Fantastic   95

19 Simon Maisey: Cov's Answer to Forrest Gump?   99

20 The Red Rose Resurrection   105

21 Like Father, Like Son?   111

22 Wearing a Tie to Help Restore the Entente Cordiale   121

23 Farewell to Coundon Road   125

24 Trying Times on the Road   131

Contributions

25 Walking With the Giants of Rugby by John Lamb   139

26 Super Seventies Revisited by Michael Austin   145

27 True As Coventry Blue by Michael Austin   153

28 Eighties Exposed: Bare bottoms, black-balling and Bermuda
    by Steve Evans   157

29 Cherished Times at Cov by Darrell Giles   163

30 The Campaigning Journalist Who Saved Cov from the Abyss
    by John Wilkinson   169

31 50 Years of Memories of Watching Cov by Alan Joseph   175

32 My Life and Times at Coventry Rugby by John Butler   181

33 Cov Were the Best Team in the Land by Brendan Gallagher   189

Players' Records

—   Introduction   197

Foreword

By Peter Rossborough (Club President)

"Cov" is, always has been, forever will be far more than a nickname, vastly greater than a sobriquet; it's a meme. It's a thought, an idea, a memory, an image of a darting break, of a massive tackle, a surging attack, a dogged, bloody-minded defence, a proudly vociferous and baying crowd, a loyalty to each other, a faith in the concept of a unification of players, supporters, sponsors and all who work tirelessly to promote endurance and success.

Cov is a meme with great transmissibility evoked by names like Juddy, Jacko, Coley, Harry, Duckers, Nobby, Gitto, Aggy, the Wheatleys, and so many more. The enduring transmissibility of this meme is enhanced by the easy interaction between all club affiliates from ballboys to internationals, from bar staff to coaches, from supporters to players. In decades to come we'll witness the emergence of another "strain" of the meme by the invocation of what Sharpy did for our club.

Memes can be paintings, a line from a play or a film, a couplet from a poem, the taste of a post-match Guinness, a memory of a great occasion, a memorable leap of ecstasy as we score, a jersey proudly worn, a programme from the 40s, an autograph secured by a young supporter, blood spilt, bones broken and so on ad infinitum.

This meme is COV in all its manifestations.

This book signals another milestone in our journey and the beginning of another 150 years!

Peter Rossborough, President

Further Foreword

A Story One Hundred and Fifty Years in the Making

By Jon Sharp (Chairman, Coventry Rugby)

It is hugely appropriate that this tribute to one of the city of Coventry's proudest symbols should touchdown between our year as UK City of Culture and the club's 150th anniversary year.

It is much more than the story of a great rugby club. It is a rich journey into the spirit of the game of rugby, the great characters who wore the blue and white hoops, the passion of its supporters, love for this club and this city, told with an easy style and the good humour that has characterised both of them through their long histories of triumph and disaster.

And who better to author this than Steve "Scribble" Evans, who spent so much time in the stands (and in the bars, it seems) recording at least the printable events as they unfolded for the readers of the *Coventry Evening Telegraph*. We are indebted to Steve who has done this as a labour of love, and indeed to all those who have contributed, with all proceeds from book sales going to the club.

'Coventry Football Club' was founded just three years after the RFU itself and gained a name as one of the most famous clubs in the world; indeed it can fairly be said to have been the greatest club in the world in its heyday of the 1960s and 70s, providing – appropriately enough for the country's centre of automotive manufacturing – a seemingly endless production line of international players.

It is worth pausing for a moment to reflect on the fact that the first ever England team to beat the All Blacks at home in New Zealand contained five of Coventry's finest (and the ref was an ex-All Black!).

The club has not been without its tribulations, but we Cov kids are used to set-backs and have always hauled ourselves up again. Now, with our solid base in the Championship, our academy system developing a string of local talent, our far-reaching community projects, our state of the art pitch and ambitious site development plans, the club is in a good place. Add into the mix the spirit, passion and love that are deep in the DNA of 'Cov', and it looks well set for the next 150.

Jon Sharp. February 2021

Jon Sharp (Chairman, Coventry Rugby)

Chapter One

Harry Walker: Mother Hen with an Equine Cavity

'**H**arry Walker, Harry Walker, Harry Walker is a horse's arse....' The unforgettable opening line to a song chorused hundreds of times by legions of players spanning the generations across the decades.

Don't for one minute assume that Harry took offence. Quite the contrary. He could often be seen at the front of the team coach, like André Previn's grandad in the orchestra pit, waving his arms about encouraging the lads to embark on a second verse.

In the pre-professional days of play-hard, shake hands and booze-hard, Harry was a rugger bugger of the highest order. And when we sang "his" song at the Cowshed Lunch to mark his 103rd birthday at the Butts Park Arena in February 2018, his grin was a gummy giveaway to the affection that was being showered upon him by more than 100 assembled ex-players.

Even the BBC cameraman recording the event started chuckling as the words became apparent. Suffice to say, the Dubbing Editor had never been busier back in the studio.

I was privileged, honoured, to cover Cov for the *Coventry Evening Telegraph* for almost a decade. And I'd dial Keresley 4842 virtually every day for team news. And the receiver would be lifted to a loud, gruff, barking response: "WALKER."

I have a theory about the day Harry was born in 1915. I'm convinced he arrived carved in granite to a thunderclap and a bolt of lightning. The city of Coventry would never be quite the same again. The man affectionately dubbed "H" had landed! Thinking about it, there could be no more fitting nick-name than "H" – the shape of rugby posts that would ultimately shape his life and his legacy.

He never knew his father, who was killed in the First World War when Harry was a baby. He was raised clinging to his mother's apron strings. She did a brilliant job and bequeathed to us, this club, this city, this county, this country, a son destined for rugby folklore.

One of Harry's best mates was the old Gloucester prop 'Digger' Morris. They locked antlers many times in blood-and-thunder battles. He loved talking about the times they knocked seven bells out of each other but, back in the clubhouse over a pint or three, they'd be long-lost brothers, despite sharing black eyes like a pair of pubescent panda bears. Digger wrote an autobiography entitled "Never Stay Down". I bought it, thanks to Harry's recommendation. It gave me an insight into just what goes on in the mysterious world of the Front Row.

In hindsight, now that Harry is lost to us forever, I wish I'd collared him and suggested ghost-writing his life's slings and arrows.

I have always put forward the theory that there is a two-inch difference between the players of the amateur and professional eras, and it has nothing to do with the size of the male appendage. Measure the distance between the heart and the wallet. Back in the day, players who came from Coventry schools like Bablake, King Henry VIII, and others, played for no monetary gain. They shared blood, sweat and beers for the pride of representing their birthplace city. T'is just my humble opinion.

Harry always led from the front, but always protected the players' backs. Even on the Bermuda Tour of 1980. We spent a month on the island and "H" organised 50cc Puch mopeds for all of us to get about. There must have been 26 of us in that blue-shirted convoy. In alphabetical terms, it was an A-Z. I looked over my shoulder and there was "H" in position Z, the tail-gunner, chugging along at the rear.

For me, it exploded the myth that a mother hen always leads its chicks. But he was leading us. In his own protective way. Watching our backs ... a mother hen cluck-clucking while chug-chugging.

Harry loved his players. We lost one of those Bermuda touring players a few years ago. Hooker Andy Farrington succumbed to cancer at an indecently young age. The lads shouldered his casket into Holy Trinity Church, Attleborough, Nuneaton, to the strains of "He Ain't Heavy, he's my brother". In the pews, I sat with Graham Robbins and Dick Travers. We blubbered like three blubbering Blubber Whales. There wasn't a dry eye in the place. Harry was outside afterwards, forlorn, head bowed. He'd lost one of his chicks.

And we have lost a mother hen, a true legend. With an equine cavity.

Harry Walker addressing a thirsty throng of former players at the annual Cowshed Lunch shortly before death at the grand old age of 103 - the oldest international on the planet.

Two legends - Harry Walker and Bill Beaumont at the Cowshed Lunch

Photos: Simon Maisey

Chapter Two

Alf Wyman: Coventry's Father Figure

He was, quite simply, a Coundon Road icon – a pre-pubescent schoolboy who grew up to become a bald-headed, bespectacled and hugely respected father figure to generations of players.

He was a spectator at the very first game ever played at Coundon Road in 1921. More than 60 years later, he would collapse and die in the clubhouse foyer.

His passing stunned the city's – and the nation's – rugby football fraternity. It was perhaps written in the stars that he should choose Coundon Road to draw his final breath. Alf probably wouldn't have wanted it any other way. Save, perhaps, having his beloved Ivy at his side.

The man who was with him during his final moments was Peter Rossborough, now the club's President.

No book about Cov would be complete without a dedication to A.A. Wyman, a Coventry clubman extraordinaire, and Peter Rossborough said: "He was known as Mr Coventry the length and breadth of the land. He was hugely respected, almost revered. He was a true father figure to everyone at the club and he commanded such respect, even from the most exalted of players."

He reflected on the night of Alf's death in the early 80s, saying: "It was a Tuesday night training session at Coundon Road. I turned up about 7pm to see Alf sitting alone in the stand. It was freezing cold.

"He'd been attending a committee meeting and complained of feeling unwell, so he went outside. I brought him back inside and we sat in the foyer. Suddenly, he just keeled over. I called 999 and the ambulance came quickly, but Alf had died."

Alf Wyman is a rare example of when the word "legend" is not misused. He is probably the most famous Cov player never to be capped – the Second World War had a big say in that respect.

A brilliant hooker, he was among a select few to pass 400 club appearances. With his distinctive, unmistakable "Chrome Dome", he was match secretary for 40 years.

Writing in the club's Centenary brochure in 1974, Alf said: "My first contact with rugby football was when Mr 'Dickie' Turland came to Stoke School in 1919 and changed the school over from soccer to rugby football. This was a great blow to me as I had been brought up to venerate Association Football.

"However, I eventually began to play rugger and managed to get into the school side and later into the England Schools' side. Through this, I started to follow the Coventry club who then played on the Coventry and North Warwickshire ground, Binley Road.

"I well remember being there and seeing the players walk into the ground in their caps and blazers. I was also present at the opening match at Coundon Road when Coventry played the United Services, Devonport. This I watched sitting on the grass under the ropes on the far side of the ground."

Alf was a gentleman, not given to revealing any outlandish antics on or off the field. But he did reveal to me one devilish snippet about his days as a hooker (the rugby position, not his nocturnal past-time) ... the match during which he claimed 20 strikes against the head.

I can't recall the opposition, but Alf said: "Their hooker only had one eye. Every time their scrum-half fed the ball in, one of our lads would cover the hooker's good eye!"

After the war, Alf was a member of the invincible Coventry team that embarked on a 72-match winning run spanning nearly four years.

He said: "That was pretty good, with a pack the average age of which was well over 30."

Writing in the club's centenary brochure, he recalled being very fortunate to be in the Coventry team that played Cardiff for the first time.

"On Boxing Day 1925, Cardiff had an open date and Coventry were able to get the fixture. Cardiff, at this time, had a two-year ground record and also very much a star-studded side, and Coventry went there and triumphed – thus starting the long association with the Cardiff club.

"This game was a great fillip to the club. Better fixtures were now possible and when you look at today's fixture list, which must be the strongest in the country, you realise how far we have come. In 1924 we had regular fixtures with Newbold, Burton, Aston Old Edwardians, the Old Edwardians, Cinderford, Stratford-on-Avon and the like."

In the 60s, the Coventry players masqueraded as Warwickshire. With one or two Cov "outsiders", the Coventry club provided virtually all the team that went on to dominate English rugby, claiming the County Championship crown seven times in eight seasons. More about that in a later chapter.

Coventry – and Warwickshire – owe a huge debt of gratitude to Alf for helping to elevate both to the dizzy summit of English rugby.

* Sincere apologies to all the great uncapped players who have served Coventry over the decades and who have not got a mention in this book. There are literally scores of them. You know who you are, chaps. Had chapters been devoted to each and every one, this book's dimensions and word-count would have rivalled Leo Tolstoy's War And Peace! Thanks to all who donned the blue-and-white, and wore it with pride and passion.

Two Coventry icons: Alf Wyman with Ivor Preece

Chapter Three

No Hiding Place for The Pimpernel

Peter Jackson's right arm hugged the ball close to his chest and, with the haste of a startled rabbit, he zig-zagged through a snarling mass of black shirts.

The New Zealand radio commentator, Winston McArthy, beautifully summed up the All Black bewilderment down on the field when he told his audience: "They seek him here, they seek him there, they seek him when he's nowhere near."

Coventry's Jackson became known as The Pimpernel on that British Lions tour of 1959, which saw him claim 16 tries in just 14 games, including four Test matches.

McArthy's astute observation captured the style and panache of Jackson the player. What it failed to do was capture the essence of Jackson the man.

Unlike many other British greats, "Jacko" refused to turn his back on the game after his retirement. Unlike the Pimpernel, there was nothing elusive about him off the field.

Coundon Road was still the place to look if anyone wished to seek him out.

I interviewed him back in 1982 – two decades after he retired – and Coventry's brilliant, legendary winger was still repaying a debt to the club that gave him so much.

"Coventry gave me more than memories. They gave me a way of life," he said. "All I'm doing it putting something back, that's all."

Putting something back – the Jackson way – meant accepting the presidency of the club and undertaking to launch a ground improvement project at Coundon Road.

Back in October 1982, Cov were preparing to meet an International XV to celebrate the official opening of a ground improvement costing £100,000. Jackson politely refused to accept the back-slaps and the plaudits.

True to form, and showing the humility that had always been his hallmark, he insisted: "It has been a great team effort."

A year earlier, after major heart surgery, he gave up the chairmanship of a sub-committee set up to mastermind the Coundon Road re-building project.

"I'd like to think that my illness pulled everyone together. Nothing comes easy in this world and everyone worked hard to make things happen. We have a lively bunch of young people coming through and they have stepped in, taken over, and gelled the club together."

That celebration match was arranged to baptise the ground improvements designed to jettison one of England's premier clubs into the 21st century ... but no-one even imagined at the time that Jackson would die in 2004 and that the fabled pasture and rickety roof of Coundon Road would be lost forever.

But, that night, there was an air of fulfilment. The work had been completed. Coundon Road had a new foyer, a Supporters' Club shop, two new dressing rooms and an attractive first-floor Sponsors' Lounge.

The club originally wanted a gymnasium, but realised it could not fit into the plans. So Cov opted for a Sponsors' Lounge in the hope that it would generate income to finance a gym at a later date.

The Coundon Road stand had been virtually untouched since Cov moved to the ground from The Butts in 1921.

I remember talking to one grey-haired supporter who told me the story of his initiation to Coundon Road as a schoolboy.

He sat in the stand with a bar of liquorice and a copy of *The Magnet* comic and waited for the surge of blue-and-white hoops to darken the green.

As he waited, a blob of water hit him on the nape of the neck. There was a hole in the roof. Years later, he returned to the ground and, in a mood of unashamed nostalgia, sought out the seat of his childhood.

Nothing had changed, he thought. And there was total confirmation when a blob of water hit him on the head!

Back then, the drops of water eventually gave way to a shower of rust particles, dislodged whenever the ball was booted onto the roof of the stand.

I remember always wearing a flat cap in the Press Box to avoid the perils of that metallic form of dandruff.

"Getting a new roof is our next priority," said Jackson. "But it takes time, and it takes money. Tonight's opening is just Phase One. It is just the beginning. There is a lot of hard work and hard fund-raising to do."

That off-the-field determination summed up the loyalty and the devotion of a man who wanted to "give back" to a club he adored.

The last thing The Pimpernel refused to do was to hide from the realisation that, even in the amateur game of the day, money was a necessary evil.

RIP Jacko. Legend.

COVENTRY FOOTBALL CLUB (R.U.)
SEASON 1959-60

Club Captain (Phil Judd) welcomes Peter Jackson on his return
from British Lion's Tour 1959

*Coventry skipper Phil Judd welcomes back clubmate Peter Jackson from the
British Lions tour of 1959-60. Autographed image by courtesy of Barrie Duckett.*

Chapter Four

Voyage of the Last Sea Lions ... with a Coventry Legend aboard Ship

Whoever organised the British Lions tour to New Zealand in 1950 had clearly done his homework. To him fell the task of transporting 30 rugby gladiators halfway across the world by sea and ensuring that, a month later, they arrived ready and primed for sporting combat against the feared and mighty All Blacks.

The four home unions decided that there should be few distractions on the trip across the Atlantic, through the Panama Canal, and into the open Pacific.

It was the last great sporting pilgrimage before jet-age travel. The last sea Lions.

So when the 15,896 tons SS Ceramic steamed out of Liverpool with the British Lions on board, there was little to occupy the minds of the players other than what awaited them Down Under. The ship was a cargo vessel catering for just 82 passengers ... and only three were women!

Coventry's Ivor Preece was on board. He was not a stowaway. He was there on merit as England's captain.

Ivor said farewell to his wife Betty and five-month-old son Peter. He would not see them again for six months.

I was privileged, no honoured, to spend an afternoon in Ivor's company in May 1983 – less than four years before this Coventry legend passed away. If you think of a Cov icon, you will think of Ivor.

This is what he told me at the time: "We spent four weeks and two days at sea and the organisers, in their wisdom, made sure we had a quiet ship. It was a little bit tedious because there wasn't a lot to do.

After we went through the Panama Canal, our only companions were the flying fish.

The touring party departed on April 1 – but they were nobody's fools.

Within 48 hours of sailing, the tour manager "Ginger" Osborne organised a whip-round among the players. With the proceeds, the Lions threw a cocktail party – traditional on long sea voyages – and invited the other 52 passengers.

Ivor told me: "It was a master stroke. Ours was the first cocktail party and, from then on, the other passengers organised their own. Naturally, they could not leave us out and we were invited to every one."

Apart from the ship's captain, there were four other "skippers" on board the Ceramic. There was Ivor (Coventry and England), Karl Mullen (Ireland), Peter Kininmonth (Scotland) and Bleddyn Williams (Wales).

They docked at Wellington on May 2 to a warm Maori welcome but Ivor said: "We needed seven days to get our land legs. We had got used to the sea-sickness but we still had to keep our eye on one or two individuals who later suffered from home-sickness. Curiously, it was always the big tough guys who suffered in that way."

The Lions had gone to New Zealand with a record which showed only one Test match win there since 1904.

It was a record which they would not improve on during the forthcoming four-match series against the All Blacks – but they won a legion of friends.

The Lions played on average every four days – they won 17 of their 18 provincial games.

Feeding the players on board a train proved a novel exercise. Orders would be taken and the guard would telephone the details to a station 50 miles ahead ... and they had to scoff their snap on the platform in just 23 minutes.

"Don't ask me why," said Ivor. "But that was always the amount of time we had to eat and get back on board."

The trip home was a contrast. They returned via Australia, Ceylon and the Suez on board the P&O ship "Strathnaver" carrying 1,100 passengers. Ivor said: "I only saw my team-mates at meal times".

After six months away – two of which were spent at sea – the party arrived at Tilbury bearing gifts for long-awaited reunions with their families. Ivor handed over a sailor doll to his son Peter, now almost a year old.

Twenty-three years later, Peter was one of five Coventry players in the England team which beat New Zealand in Auckland.

But that's another story.

He roared for Coventry, England and the Lions
... Ivor Preece in his British Lions jersey

Chapter Five

Seven Glorious Years During the Reign of King Cole

Beneath an imposing palm tree, George Cole sported a snazzy polka-dot hat and shielded his legs with a beach towel. Away from the searing Bermudian sunshine on Trunk Island in Harrington Sound, he looked a proper Petunia, slurping unashamedly on a fast-melting ice cream dripping down the cone and between his fingers.

For probably the only time in his career. George had found himself in the shade. It was a time to reflect.

The man who broke appearances and points records for both Coventry and Warwickshire was, in 1980, no more than an assistant manager on Coventry's "fun" tour of Bermuda.

The prince of place-kickers, crowned 'King Cole' by numerous headline-writers, was now in splendid abdication with a highly productive left boot reduced to kicking sand.

His reluctance to face the sun destroyed my theory that George was a scrum-half powered by solar energy during a playing career which saw ageless skills blossom beyond his 40th year.

His memories back then seemed to be harnessed to the elements. I remember asking him about the first County Championship Final he ever played in and he replied: "Oh yes, I remember that one. There was sunshine, snow and rain. We had the lot that day."

It was March 8, 1958, and West Countrymen by the train-load steamed north to turn Coundon Road into a Cornish Riviera.

Warwickshire (with a huge influx of Cov players) beat Cornwall 16-8 but George, who kicked two conversions and a penalty, remembered the match not because of what happened on the field. "It was the atmosphere that struck me. All those Cornishmen, smashing people, who had got up at 4am to travel up. When we went to the Hotel Leofric for the after-match meal, the city seemed to be full of them waiting for their trains back at midnight." They were scenes which George and the rest of the squad would grow accustomed to. The celebrations that night triggered a chain reaction which saw Warwickshire write one of the most remarkable chapters in the history of the County Championship.

In eight glorious seasons between 1958 and 1965, Warwickshire took the title seven times to stand at the pinnacle of English rugby.

George was destined to hitch a permanent joy-ride as the Coventry-inspired bandwagon rolled on relentlessly. George Cole, Stan Purdy and Phil Judd were the only players to appear in all seven finals.

The following year, they had to travel to Bristol to meet mighty Gloucestershire in the final. They emerged 14-9 victors.

Two titles on the trot and Surrey were the obstacle standing between Warwickshire and their hat-trick in 1960. George jubilantly fired over an angled penalty from the Coundon Road touchline to earn a 9-6 verdict.

Phil Judd, Bert Godwin and Mike McLean, the all-Coventry front-row, had claimed more than 30 strikes against the head in one Midland Group match against Staffordshire. Their names rolled off the tongue with the same ease with which opponents were shunted backwards.

Peter Jackson, the Warwickshire captain, described the pack as the best he had ever played with. "They inspired awe ... they really were something to behold," said the Coventry, England and British Lions winger.

Ray Batstone, the Coventry flanker, said he was able to postpone his retirement only because his body was spared punishment by the

Warwickshire "front five". Playing behind them he insisted, offered complete protection.

As scrum-half, Cole had a fairly predictable role. He simply fed the ball into the tunnel and waited for it to emerge at the feet of John Gardiner, his No 8. It was almost boringly straight-forward.

With ball-winning such a snip, match-winning was a formality and the legions of Coventry and Warwickshire folk were justifiably confident about the 1961 campaign.

It turned out to be a bitter anti-climax.

Warwickshire failed even to take the regional title, losing 10-9 to East Midlands in a Midland Group play-off at Coundon Road which, years later, continued to haunt the legendary Peter Jackson.

Jackson told me: "I made a very grave error that night and it remains a vividly horrible memory among so many happy ones."

Warwickshire were leading with the minutes ticking away when 'Jacko' fielded the ball on his own goal-line.

He recalled: "We were under tremendous pressure and I had dropped back to help out. I collected the ball over our try-line and tried to clear, but the angle wasn't quite right and, anyway, I wasn't one of the world's best kickers.

"So, I tried to run the ball out. I remember being tackled. A lot of pent-up energy went into that tackle and I was literally driven into the ground. The ball went loose and one of their players dropped onto it and claimed the try.

The crowd were stunned. Northampton's Don White, knowing that his conversion would win the match, used typical flamboyance to silence the terrace barracking. He actually sat on the ball and waited until the hooting subsided. Then he landed the kick and Warwickshire were out.

"I was terribly, terribly dejected," said Jackson. "The enormity of the error was made worse because I was the captain."

Warwickshire, though, bounced back to beat Hampshire in the Twickenham final a year later and, in 1963, made it five titles in six years by overcoming Yorkshire 13-10 at Coundon Road.

Lancashire surrendered 8-6 in the 1964 final and Warwickshire travelled to Hartlepool a year later to beat Durham 15-9 and collected their seventh title in eight seasons.

By now, though, the ravages of time had systematically eroded the strength of Warwickshire's once-feared pack. Coventry's Godwin, McLean and Gardiner had gone.

It was the end of an era. Their stranglehold on English rugby had loosened with the march of time.

Not even George Cole, a Peter Pan among players, could prevent the sun setting on a Warwickshire career which brought him a record 87 caps and 539 points. He failed to score in only five games and his county career, spanning the years 1954-1972, ended at the age of 38.

FOOTNOTE: *It can be a perilous job being a place-kicker. George recalled a match at Kingsholm, playing for Cov against Gloucester. He needed to slot over a last-minute penalty virtually in front of the posts to win the match. The partisan crowd cheered when the ball hit the upright. Within a split second, George plunged them into silence by collecting the rebound and dropping a goal. As he left the pitch in triumph at the final whistle, an old lady clobbered him on the head with her umbrella!*

SIMPLY THE BEST: "King Cole"

IMMORTALISED: There are apartments now on the site of Coundon Road. One is named in honour of George Cole. Photo: Alan Joseph

Majestic Cov

Chapter Six

Bottoms Up ... or Southern Points Northwards

A TRIBUTE TO JIM BRODERICK AND THE COV FRONT-ROW UNION

In the golden slip-stream of David Duckham's flowing blond locks, they were often left clutching the leg of a shadow. Tackling Duckham in a one-against-one confrontation was always a mesmeric experience. If the hypnotic side-step failed, the electric pace was guaranteed to stun.

It was the same when Peter Jackson took them on.

Pale-faced Peter was known as The Cadavar because he looked like death both before and during a game. He was also nicknamed Nicolai the Spy because, apparently, he slept with one eye open.

A gush of air, a ghostly swerve and the athletic apparition was gone, scampering gleefully towards the line with not so much a cursory glance over its shoulder.

It was skill that chilled spectators and style that chastened opponents.

Together, Jackson and Duckham shared 274 tries in separate careers spanning three decades of wing wizardry at Coundon Road. There were others, like Nobby Bolton, Tim Barnwell, Paul Knee and Simon Maisey.

Such brilliant performers have now passed into legend, of course, but their often spectacular, always special contributions linger in the memories of all who looked on in awe and admiration.

Sights to behold and tries to cherish, though, have not always been the exclusive copyright of star threequarters at Coventry.

Those who prefer the broadsword to the sabre – blunt-edged forwards rather than incisive backs – have found plenty to savour.

From the Wheatley brothers, Harry Walker, through the Godwin-Judd-McLean era to Johnson-Brain-Wilkes, the Cov front row has been successfully bred with a handsome pedigree.

In the early 70s, Coventry were involved in a match which, from a forward's point of view, has long since passed into Coundon Road folklore.

It was a John Player Cup-tie at Orrell, whose youthful pack had foolishly involved themselves in pre-match banter which got a lot of Press coverage.

They pointed the finger especially at Jim Broderick and Keith Fairbrother, the two Coventry props, slurring them with labels like "has-beens" and "old men".

The crowd at Edge Hall Road braced themselves in anticipation. Would youth conquer experience? Or would the men teach the boys a spanking good lesson?

What followed during the next 80 minutes can best be described as a slaughter of the innocents.

Nothing encourages a side more than to see their opponents being shunted backwards in the scrums. In this case, Orrell's eight-man unit not only surrendered yardage in frantic retreat, but their front-row was unceremoniously hoisted skywards at virtually every put-in.

Broderick, 386 appearances in a blue and white jersey, remembered the match with relish.

He was captain for the day because Duckham had cried off. "It was tremendous," said Brodders. "Throughout the match, the feet of their front row were parallel with our eyes in the scrums. I'm not exaggerating. They were airborne every time."

Propping down that day opposite Broderick was Orrell's teenager, Sammy Southern, who went on to become Orrell's captain a decade later.

Broderick, who worked at Dunlop's Aviation Division in Coventry, seized devilishly on the "flying lesson" theme.

He said at the time: "If you speak to Master Southern over the next few days, ask him if he wants any wings sending up."

The words were not meant to intimidate. They merely offered Southern a reminder of his fiery introduction to the rigours of front-row combat.

Mud-spattered forwards have often referred to the clean-shirted backs as "girlies" while, in retort, the forwards are perceived as grunt-and-moan merchants.

There is, however, and always will be, a massive respect for what goes on in the mysterious and devilish world of the Front Row Union.

Bottoms up, Mr Southern!

Jim Broderick JP
'Brodders'

Chapter Seven

Boom! Evans above, It's "Bomber"

Contrary to devilish myth, "Bomber" Evans had nowt to do with the war-time crater scarring the Coundon Road pitch, leaving the Wheatley brothers to use strong arms and shovels to fill the void.

But, now in his 85th year, he recalls with relish being responsible for a blistering attack which left the city of Cambridge in sporting shell-shock.

It earned him the rare accolade of a cartoon appearing in The Pink to mark his devastating arrival in an RAF jersey – three tries and three conversions on his debut against Cambridge University just three days after launching his military service.

Roy "Bomber" Evans left an indelible impression, too, on his beloved birthplace city of Coventry, turning out 226 times for Cov and scoring 70 tries. He was an awesome back-row forward among a cluster of scrummaging tail-gunners gracing Coundon Road across the decades. And a lovely bloke, t'boot.

In a proud manufacturing city which attracted the unwanted attention of the Luftwaffe during the war, Roy emerged from the productive conveyor belt of Dunlop along with players like George Cole, David Dove, Ray Batstone, Bob Frame and Jim Broderick, to name just a few.

He joined Cov in the mid-50s and retired in 1970, later being endowed with the much-deserved honour of club president.

It was the legendary talent-spotter Harry Walker who brought him to Cov. "He asked me to turn out for the Extras. In my opinion, Coventry

Extras were the second best team in Warwickshire. So many great players waiting for their chance in the first team."

After his call-up to the RAF, he was selected for the Combined Services against Ireland in Belfast. He was a brutal tackler. "When I tackled a player, I flattened him," he said. "I acquired that skill at Dunlop.

"While in the Air Force, I actually played against Cov – and we beat them!"

Back in the Cov fold after his two-year RAF stint, he especially revered No 8 John Gardiner and Ray Batstone. "They looked after me," he said. It was a small sentence that spoke a thousand words.

Roy and his adoring, ever supportive wife, Jill, have been married for more than half-a-century. When they met, Jill had never seen a rugby match. She was a Sky Blues fan and a regular at Highfield Road during the Jimmy Hill era.

Jill, now a long-serving rugby convert, smiles when she looks back on Bomber's playing days – and his thighs!

Bomber used to trim his shorts in a way that almost certainly influenced Nick Jeavons, dubbed in the 80s as the Male Model of Moseley.

Bomber's fashion statement of the Swinging Sixties led to one Cov supporter penning a three-stanza poem which he or she anonymously sent to the club selectors. Jill has kept that poem all these years and it still makes her chuckle. It goes like this:

We're not asking them to reach the knee
But may a member make a plea?
We're partial to a bit of thigh
But Evans' shorts are just too high.

BOOM! Evans above, It's "Bomber"

At No 8 in the back row
The loops of jock-strap hanging low
He reminds us of the bird from Leek
Who had her periods twice a week.

Can't Cov supply a longer pair for free
Or Bomber wear his straps internally?
Some action, take. Oh, be a chum!
It puts us off to see his bum!!!

Despite Bomber's excellent try-scoring exploits wearing short-shorts, one score sticks in his mind. "We were playing against Rugby at Webb Ellis Road and we were losing by two points towards the end. I had never tried a drop-goal before, but I went for it and the ball cleared the crossbar by two centimetres and we won."

He has fond memories of the brilliant George Cole: "A fabulous scrum-half and a great kicker. In those days at the line-out, we were allowed to link arms to prevent the opposition getting through to target our scrum-half. George always managed to find touch but, on one occasion, he sliced his kick and it hit Dave Dove right in the balls and he collapsed on the ground!

"There was another game in the mud at Cardiff when there was a bit of hand-bagging and all the shirts were filthy. The ref blew up and awarded a scrum. Cardiff had nine in their pack and we only had seven. One of our lads had wrongly packed down with them because all the jerseys looked the same."

Players of all generations have off-the-field stories to tell. They have always got up to mischief. None more so than the Cov team enjoying an overnight stay in a Swansea hotel in the Sixties.

Much-lamented Alf Wyman was the match secretary on the trip. Bomber recalls with relish: "Ray Batstone was a devil. He found out that the doors to our rooms all had rising hinges, so we took all the doors off and placed them in Alf's room. He had 13 doors on his bed."

After Bomber and Jill got married, they moved to live in Wolvey – right next door to Pauline and Jim Broderick. The two couples were firm friends as well as fabulous neighbours.

It gutted Bomber when Brodders died. "We got a reduction in rates moving next door to Brodders," joked Bomber. "He was a great friend and I was a pall-bearer at his funeral."

He recalls, before marriage and living in Foleshill, the times he and Phil Judd caught the train from Foleshill Station to Coundon Road. "The train fare was just 4d – and on away games of more than 40 miles Alf Wyman used to give us three half-crowns, about 37p in today's money, for expenses."

Looking back, Bomber does not regret a moment of his time with Cov, which started in the 50s and continued into the 70s.

"One thing I will never forget is how proud I was to play for Cov. They were one of the best clubs in the land and everything you got, you had to earn.

"You had to play 12 games in a season to earn a players' tie and 20 games to earn a blazer badge – not 18, not 19, but 20. I am so proud of that club."

BOOM! Evans above, It's "Bomber"

Bomber with his rugby-playing grandson, Oscar

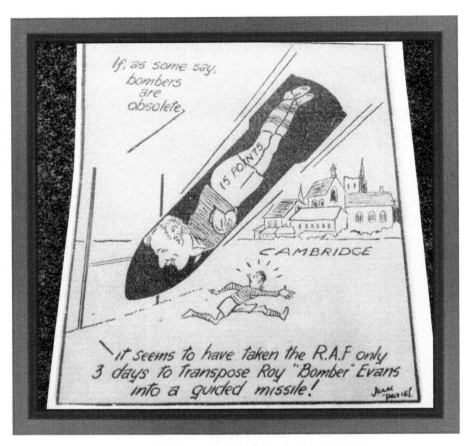

A cartoon marking Bomber's devastating debut for the RAF

Chapter Eight

Wing Wizard Centurions

For a man named Webb, it was spookily ordained that he should make his Coventry debut against a player with Ellis among his christian names.

Not even the Rugby Football gods could have conjured a Webb-Ellis man-to-man confrontation.

Rodney 'Sam' Webb was born in Newbold, not far from the game's birthplace. His Cov baptism saw him pitched against Dewi Iorworth Ellis Bebb, the brilliant Welsh winger who won 34 caps.

In the dressing room before that Swansea-Coventry fixture, Cov skipper Phil Judd looked at his debut-maker and said: "You will be marking No. 14."

Webb replied: "No I won't."

Judd, taken aback, insisted: "I said you will be marking their No. 14."

Again, Webb countered: "No I won't." Then he added: "Their No. 14 will be marking me!"

It wasn't arrogance. It was the defiant confidence of a man who would enjoy a glittering Coventry career of wing wizardry yielding more than 100 club tries and earn him 12 England caps – and a try against Scotland on his international debut in 1967. Clubmate Phil Judd was his England skipper that day.

His career also embraced Warwickshire, the Midlands and the Barbarians.

It is true to say that "Sam" Webb would go on to play a huge, massive part in promoting the appeal of the oval-ball game, both at home and abroad. His firm made the hand-stitched Gilbert match balls and, in 1985, he opened the Rugby Football Museum in St Matthews Street which boosts the town of Rugby's tourism trade, attracting 30.000 visitors a year.

There were six boys in the Webb family and four of them played rugby. His brother Richard ended up playing for Australia. "He came over on tour and we both played against each other in a Midlands v Australia game," said Sam. "Between us, me and Richard scored all the points in that game."

He looks back at his time at Coundon Road with pride. "In my early days at Cov, the England selectors relied on the Oxbridge players, but Cov broke that mould. Even Wales looked to Coventry. Ron Jones could not get a cap, but even the Welsh selectors started to look towards Coventry and Ron won his caps.

"Alf Wyman ran Cov and he did a good job. He used to give me five bob (25p) for my petrol expenses.

"I remember the Scotland lads had to pay 17/6d (75p) for their international jerseys. That was a lot of money back in those days."

So, how did Rodney Webb get the nickname "Sam"? He was given it by his father.

"My dad always called me Sam. Apparently, it comes from a war-time poem about a lad called Sam and his musket."

It actually comes from 'Sam, Sam, Pick Oop Tha' Musket', a music hall monologue by Stanley Holloway.

He recalls a friendly rivalry with fellow Coventry winger Ricky Melville.

"The *Daily Telegraph* used to publish a weekly list of the country's top try-scorers. Me and Ricky were both at the top.

"He came over to me and said 'Webby, I'm nearing the end of my career – put me over for a try or two.' So I did – and he ended up playing for another three seasons or so!

"One of the things Ricky would do was dribble the ball from sometimes 25 yards out and score a try. I used to think he was a jammy bugger for doing that, but he'd do it year after year. It was sheer skill."

Ricky Melville, who died in 2012, was untouchable in the Fifties and Sixties. To this day, he holds records which may never be surpassed. His hair was so immaculately groomed that some called him The Brylcreem Boy.

He made 386 appearances for the club and scored 281 tries – a record, and the only player to top the 200 mark. In the 1960-61 season, he ran in 45 tries, again a record.

Another much-lamented Coventry centurion winger was Nobby Bolton, who died in Australia in 2008. He played for the club in the 60s and 70s, scoring 122 tries.

Other ton-up wingers like Peter Jackson, David Duckham and Simon Maisey are celebrated in other chapters, but the Webb-Ellis 'name game' that launched this particular chapter will end with a player whose name ended up being a prophetic curse.

Paul Knee was on the verge of an England call-up when he broke his arm. The winger who captained Cov in the early 80s had enjoyed a productive decade – but it was plagued by injury.

I recall Ken Widdows, the Sports Editor at the *Coventry Evening Telegraph*, dispatching photographer Bob Cole to Coundon Road in the hope of snapping Knee's 100th try for the club.

Bob took up his position behind the dead-ball line and clicked away. Knee duly delivered his landmark score. Bob Cole arrived in the office on the following Monday morning to be confronted by a scowling Sports Editor who did not like the photograph.

"But Paul ran straight at me," protested Bob.

A few months later, after yet another knee operation, the centurion winger would be forced to hang up his boots.

A poorly knee had signalled the end for Paul Knee.

*****

THE XV WHO ARE MEMBERS OF THE "CENTURIONS CLUB":

Ricky Melville wing 281 tries
Harold Greasley wing 181
David Duckham wing/centre 147
Ivor Preece fly-half 135
Peter Jackson wing 127
Nobby Bolton wing 122
George Harriman centre 121
Graham Robbins No8 118
Rod Webb wing 118
Simon Maisey wing 110
Peter Rossborough full-back 109
John Gardiner No8 107
Paul Knee wing 105
Peter Preece centre 104

Wing wizard centurions ... Ricky Melville and Rodney 'Sam' Webb.
This dynamic duo shared 399 Coventry tries

Chapter Nine

Dai for Cov, England and the British Lions

He arrived at Barkers' Butts Lane with enough pocket money for bus fare and, years later, was destined to leave to a fanfare. The No. 5 Corporation bus carried an unambitious, fresh-faced kid who turned up unannounced for midweek training at Coundon Road.

He went to the ground because his mentor at Old Coventrians RFC, Bob Holland, had taken him aside and told him bluntly and honestly: "You are far too good for us. Get yourself down to Cov and join them."

It was the launch of a playing career that would embrace Coventry, Warwickshire, the Barbarians, England and the British Lions.

David Duckham was a kid brought up on the playground at Coundon Infants and Junior School and the playing field of King Henry VIII School but he had no burning rugby ambitions as a teenager.

"I was about 13 when I saw my first Cov match," he recalls. "We got free tickets as schoolkids and I was mesmerised when I saw Peter Jackson play. I just lived for the moment he got the ball. He was my hero, my idol. He literally took my breath away."

Duckham was not coached as a youngster. Totally inspired by Jackson, he would practice his swerves and side-steps.

"I was not the quickest but I used to get away with it by stealth," he said. "I loved the sideways movements of Peter Jackson and my heart used to race when he got the ball.

"I wasn't ambitious and I didn't really enjoy my rugby at Old Coventrians. Bob Holland was a father figure to me at OC's and he took me to one side and told me to join Cov.

"So I turned up on the bus, thinking that Bob had telephoned the club, but I don't think he had. I just turned up and they let me train with them."

The rest is history, glorious history.

Duckham recalls that, when he arrived, several Cov players were away on an England tour to Canada. He got to meet them when they returned.

Phil Judd was one of them. "When I first met him, I said 'Hello Mr Judd," said Duckham. "I was in awe of all the players but Phil was very nice and told me not to call him Mister. I was only three years out of school at the time and they were all heroes to me."

In his first season with Cov, he says he "got away with blue murder and trickery". His natural style hoodwinked opponents and left spectators gasping. In fact, recalls Duckham, the rugby correspondent at the *Birmingham Post*, Michael Blair. even wrote that the young, uncapped Duckham was so talented that he should be selected for the British Lions! That honour would come later.

Duckham has fond memories of two Cov players during his early days – Tony Holt and Alan James.

"Tony Holt's nickname was Titch. He always used to chew gum and one day in the dressing room, he called me Quackers. He suddenly came out with it. Jim Broderick latched onto it immediately and they even called me Ducks."

He was particularly in awe of fly-half Alan James. "He was a graceful runner, one of the best sellers of a dummy I have ever seen. He was a great player and we had a great relationship on the field. He would have won a fistful of caps but he lost interest in the game."

There is one match that lingers long in Duckham's memory and those of rugby-lovers across the British Isles and beyond. There is a reel of celluloid never allowed to gather dust at Shepherds Bush. It is footage of the Baa Baa's match against New Zealand at Cardiff in 1973.

Playing the game according to the run-with-it doctrine of William Webb Ellis, the Barbarians – and Duckham – produced a performance against a full Test side that will remain etched on the souls of fans worldwide.

During one trademark Duckham dash, the dancing feet even sold a dummy to the BBC cameraman recording the match. The cameraman panned right as Duckham swerved left!

He looks back with huge pride and affection.

"The intensity and drama of the occasion was almost overwhelming. The tension was truly remarkable, the like of which I had never experienced before or after. Some of the game's keen onlookers have even suggested this was my finest ever performance on a rugby field. I would not argue."

He was the only Englisman in a glittering back division. After the game, the Cardiff crowd and the Welsh fans christened him "Dai". They were convinced that playing as he did, he must have been a Welshman. Duckham accepts it as the best compliment a Coventry kid and a proud Englishman could receive.

He said: "The traditionalism of the Barbarians' concept is a reminder of how the game should be played. My own example is surely a worthy example for it was only when I wore their colours that I was able to see the light of day as far as my role on the field was concerned."

At King Henry VIII School, he studied the classics, like Greek and Latin. Well, one Latin phrase springs to mind – Carpe Diem, which means *seize the day*. Duckham certainly seized it with both feet that day.

He looks back on his Coventry career with pride. "I was damned lucky to play for Cov and to captain the club for two seasons. We had 14 internationals and it was a hell of an experienced team. I was part of it, more by luck than judgement. They were the best club in the country in my opinion."

The abolition of the grammar schools and the demise of works' teams in a once-productive city has, in Duckham's opinion, contributed to the loss of the conveyor belt of home-grown talent.

Sport has a tendency to throw up its icons and idols. In the 70s, soccer had Pelé and George Best. I would argue that David Duckham fits snugly into the oval-ball category of post-war legends.

He picked up the ball and he ran with it. Gleefully and gloriously.

The Coventry kid who dipped into his pocket money for bus fare was destined to leave to a Buckingham Palace fanfare.

After his retirement, he was awarded an MBE for his services to rugby. It was his deserved, crowning glory.

DAVID DUCKHAM – an all-time England "great"

His name will live on. The fabled field at Coundon Road,
where he thrilled thousands, now adopts his name.
Photo: Alan Joseph

43

Majestic Cov

Chapter Ten

Twing & Twang - the Dynamic Coventry Duo

The cherubic smile masked a burning desire to do well at sport. As an angelic Coventry choirboy, he was destined to pull on the cherished, rose-endowed jersey of England and grace the greenery of Twickenham – the High Church of our beloved game.

He would even go on to pull on the blood-red attire of the British Lions.

Geoff Evans was a multi-gifted sporting all-rounder who garnished his first headline at the tender age of 10 ... playing soccer.

Turning out in the Coventry Choiristers League with his fellow choirboys, they won a match 18-0 – and Geoff scored 10 of them.

The achievement earned him a small piece in the *Coventry Evening Telegraph*'s Pink edition under the headline of "GOOD EVANS!"

He went on to become the English Schools' long-jump champion, leaping 22 feet, before turning his blossoming talent to rugby ... and winning a shilling (5p) in an unorthodox high-jump challenge.

Training on the Bablake School playing fields, Geoff stood between the posts and kept leaping up and down hoping to touch the crossbar.

His Bablake rugby master, Mr Morgan, told him: "If you can touch the crossbar, I'll give you a shilling."

The gauntlet was down. Suffice to say, the thought of such an incentive put an extra spring in his step and the coin was jubilantly clinched. Maybe his leaping prowess influenced his debut for the school rugby team – as a second-row forward, packing down alongside a pubescent Rob Fardoe, destined to become his Coventry team-mate at Coundon Road.

But it was with another Coventry schoolboy that Geoff would forge an immortal alliance as a centre-threequarter. His name was Peter Preece and both would be at the heartbeat of the England team, between them sharing 21 caps.

Peter, the proud son of Ivor, a Coventry player who captained England, maintained a glowing family dynasty (his son, Adam, played for Leamington, Broadstreet and Warwickshire).

Peter said: "Easily, the best centre I ever played with was Geoff Evans. And John Spencer was special, too."

In the Coventry dressing room, they were known as Twing and Twang.

Geoff explains: "We were always either pulling a muscle or pulling a hamstring. Even on the England tours, whenever the trainer came on, he'd say 'Don't drink the water. Spit it out. Don't drink it.' I'm sure that's why we suffered so much with pulled muscles. My earliest memories of the Cov dressing room were of Harry Prosser and Bill Gittings walking around smoking fags while we were getting changed."

While studying at Manchester University, Geoff turned out a dozen or so times for Sale. They offered him the captaincy to stay on. But Geoff turned to someone he regarded as his "rugby dad" – Billy Gittings – for advice.

"I always regarded Billy as my rugby dad. I asked him what I should do and he said to come back to Cov. For the last two years at university, I travelled back to play for Cov in my Sunbeam Alpine, then my Triumph Vitesse and eventually my Cortina GT."

After a night out as a student, he returned to his digs at silly o'clock to receive the message: "Telephone home immediately – You have been selected for England's tour to the Far East".

Geoff said: "It included Japan, Singapore and Ceylon. I played in 5 or 6 games for England when caps weren't awarded. Jim Broderick was on that tour and played against Japan, but he got badly injured and came home on a stretcher from memory."

There was one tour to Fiji and New Zealand that Cov's dynamic duo vividly recall.

Peter said: "We were training in Fiji and there was an almighty thunderstorm. Suddenly, the pitch was full of thousands and thousands of frogs."

Geoff recalls: "That was amazing. You just couldn't walk for frogs, everywhere, all over the pitch and the running track. But we still thrashed Fiji 13-12 … !"

The Evans-Preece centre pairing was never more rejoiced in Coventry than in 1973 at Eden Park, Auckland. They were joined in the England ranks that day by Peter Rossborough, David Duckham and Fran Cotton – making it a Cov quality quintet. A third of the team, proud to pull on the blue-and-white of Coventry at club level and then represent their country, they went on to become the first England team to beat the All Blacks in their own back yard.

Geoff particularly recalls one John Player Cup match against Gloucester in 1973. As Cup-holders, they were drawn to meet Gloucester at Coundon Road. The cherry-and-whites clearly had a plan to prevent the ball reaching a virtually all-international Coventry back division.

Within 20 minutes of the kick-off, Gloucester ensured the ball to the backs was severed at source. They targeted scrum-half Billy Gittings and laid him out. Deliberate or accidental? We will never know.

Geoff recalls: The match ended 6-all. We didn't realise we had actually lost. We thought there would be a replay, but Gloucester went through as the away team."

But back to the England fold. Geoff revealed how the international team escaped what would have been a catastrophic incident after a 12-all draw against France at the Parc des Princes. And it was all because of the play-hard, booze-hard camaraderie of the rugby brotherhood.

After the game, Geoff and his team-mates went out to enjoy the Paris nightlife. They had been booked to return home on a flight from Orly airport the next morning. Hung over, they missed the flight.

Turkish Airlines flight 981, a DC-10, due to fly from Orly to Heathrow, crashed shortly after take-off on March 3, 1974, killing all 346 passengers and crew on board. It was, at the time, the worst crash in aviation history.

Geoff refuses to dwell on it, saying: "We didn't know anything about the Paris Air Disaster, but we were told when we got back to ring our families to let them know we were safe. Everyone was killed on that flight, including the entire Bury St Edmunds rugby team. That might have been us."

He and Peter Preece, Twing and Twang, the dynamic duo, both look back on their cherished – and charmed – careers with a sense of glorious gratitude.

"I was so very lucky, so lucky," said Geoff. "Rugby is all about the people you meet, people like Peter Preece, Peter Rossborough, David Duckham, Billy Gittings. I was very, very lucky to play alongside those lads."

Peter Preece, Geoff Evans and Peter Rossborough – three Cov legends who were part of the England XV who beat the All Blacks in their own back yard in 1973 – with lifelong supporter Alan Joseph (second from right).

Photo: Janet Joseph

Chapter Eleven

A Bunch of Woven Red Roses for 'Rosie'

There was a time when nearly every name on the Coventry team-sheet was followed by an asterisk, a tiny typographical star denoting twinkling talents that lit up international arenas from Auckland to the Arms Park.

It was a time, too, when red roses flourished at Coundon Road — their roots embedded deep in more than a dozen Coventry hearts.

That proud emblem of English rugby achievement, sewn on dazzling white, blossomed more than ever in the city during the early 70s.

Some, like the dashing Duckham, were handed what amounted to bouquets. Others, like Gittings and Ninnes, were given a derisory but no less cherished single stem.

One by one, the names passed into Coventry folklore until, somewhat fittingly, a player nicknamed 'Rosie' became the last of that far from fragile red rose brigade of the glorious Seventies.

When Peter Rossborough announced his retirement in 1984, it was the end of an era. Coventry's largely home-grown England internationals like Gittings, Duckham, Preece, Cowman, Evans, Creed, Fairbrother, Wardlow, Barton, Webb and Cotton had already gone. So, too, had Ron Jones (Wales).

Now a grandfather of four, it is a time to reflect for Rossborough. He harbours fond memories of fabulous players and fine people spanning so many epic seasons.

At 19, when he made his senior debut for Cov in the forbidding yet fantastic Cardiff Arms Park, the physical and psychological appetites were fierce. So, too, was the ambition.

Four years later, Rossborough returned to the Dragon's lair to make his England debut against Wales. It was a highlight that turned harshly sour. He wore a woven red rose on his heart, but he wore his heart on his sleeve after an error brutally punished.

"We lost 22-6 and although that was the best result England had had down there for several seasons, I was dropped. So was Barry Ninnes, my Coventry clubmate who was also making his debut. It was dreadful for 'Basil' because he never got back in.

"That was the low spot of my career. I felt for 'Basil' and I was in despair. That soon became a resolve to win back my place."

Television highlights of that game repeatedly showed Rossborough failing to hold an up-and-under. The ball was stolen and Gerald Davies went in for a try.

"It was the only one I dropped," said the former Coventry full-back. "I'd held the other 10 or 12 that came my way but that's all history now and there's no point dwelling on it."

It took a determined and defiant Rossborough two years to win back his England place for a match that left every member of the squad in tears. This time, though, there was no despair.

The venue was Eden Park, Auckland, and, for the first time in rugby history England had beaten the mean, mighty and magnificent All Blacks in their own back yard.

Rossborough kicked two conversions in an historic 16-10 victory. It triggered tears of triumph.

"There were 20 grown men just crying in each other's arms," he said. "We had lost the three provincial games in the build-up to the Test and everyone had written us off but we played our hearts out that day."

From John Watkins alone, the big, brave Gloucester forward, there were enough tears to fill a dozen empty champagne bottles. "He didn't stop crying for 20 minutes," recalls Rossborough. "The emotion of the occasion was just incredible."

The fact that there were four other Coventry players on that so-memorable occasion – Duckham, Preece, Evans and Cotton – ensured a cherished place in Rossborough's lengthy list of magic rugby moments.

He cherishes, too, those days when he donned the blue-and-white hoops of Cov at a time when they boasted so many internationals.

"There was no sense of big-headedness nor arrogance. There was just a tremendous confidence in the side. Fourteen of us could have a mediocre game but it just needed the remaining player to turn it on and we would win. And when all of us clicked together, well, we would run up a cricket score."

In the early 70s when Cov twice won the Knock-Out Cup, later sponsored by John Player, there was an all-international line-up behind the scrum.

It was no secret that the opposition would set out to neutralise that threat by depriving Cov's silky runners of the ball. And that meant stemming the flow at source ... by hammering the scrum-half.

Bill Gittings was invariably the player singled out.

"It didn't bother Bill when they flew into him," said Rossborough. "He just picked himself up and laughed. He was as hard as nails and tackled anything that moved – a classic scrum-half in my opinion.

"I remember one game against Cardiff at the Arms Park in my early days. Cardiff had Gareth Edwards and Barry John at half-back and we had 'Gitto' and Alan James.

"Gitto completely outplayed Edwards and, if you look back, try and find out how many times Edwards came to Coundon Road to play after that? There weren't many. Edwards didn't fancy his chances against Bill."

Rossborough is proud to have played alongside some great players, too numerous to list, but he singles out Jim Broderick ("a special kind of man") and Barry Ninnes ("I love the bloke").

He also has fond memories of men off the field – like Harry Goodman, the Coventry and England trainer or "sponge man"; Alf Wyman and Harry Walker – two men who became mother hens to the players.

During his career, Rossborough became the only player in Coventry's history to do the double of 100 tries and 2,000 points.

When I mentioned to Simon Maisey that I was going to interview Peter Rossborough, Simon couldn't resist a chuckle and said: "Don't forget to remind him that I got one more try than him."

I mentioned it to Rossborough and he retorted: "Yes, we were both in a race to see who was first to get 100 tries. 'Daisy' won it ... but 99 of his tries came from passes from me!"

He enjoyed that little clubmate banter but he has an open dislike of statistics. Rugby, he says, is not about compiling statistics in a record book but about friends gathered around a clubhouse bar. And yes, Simon, he includes you in that guzzling gathering.

Rossborough stressed: "I got more pleasure out of making a good tackle than I ever did out of scoring a try. I get more satisfaction from the people in the game than from the points I scored."

After his retirement, he remained involved with the game he "grudgingly" embraced as a first-former at Coventry's King Henry VIII School. He attended Howes Junior School in Cheylesmore – a soccer-loving school.

"I was a bit of a naughty boy at that age and loved football but I passed my 11-plus exam and ended up at King Henry VIII. I was absolutely determined to carry on playing soccer but didn't fancy getting punished at a rugby-playing school."

His daughters, Rachael and Emma, have given him and his wife, Sandra, four lovely grandchildren – Jack, Summer, Freya and Finlay. "Jack is 13 and loves his football," said Rossborough. "Sadly, he supports Aston Villa!"

Affable and articulate, his association with Cov did not end when he hung up his boots, He went into coaching roles with Cov, the Midlands, England 7s among others and even travelled abroad in various coaching roles, as far afield as Australia and Canada.

He was coach and manager of the England A team from 1992 to 1997, including managing the full England tour to Canada; managing the England 7's to victory in the inaugural World Cup in 1993 and was a selector on the victorious British Lions team to South Africa in 1997.

He is probably the only Cov man to have been supporter, player, captain, coach, director, chairman and president.

"I was away so much in my playing days, leaving Sandra at home, that the six-week coaching trips abroad enabled me to take my family with me."

Rugby football – and Coventry – still oozes from his soul. He is in his 12th year as club president.

When we did our pre-arranged 11am telephone interview during a Corona-virus Sabbath lockdown, Rossborough and his good lady were preparing to welcome Rachael and two of the grandkids for a Sunday dinner in their family bubble. Or was it bauble?

The call was made just in time to spare grandad 'Rosie' the chore of peeling the spuds. But what a player. What an elegant, eloquent player.

Peter Rossborough - a brilliant full-back

A precious hug for daughter Emma from Peter Rossborough who sacrificed a lot of cherished family time to pursue his rugby career.

Chapter Twelve

The Preacher Who Knocked a Wheel off a Welsh Wagon

On the Sabbath, he was a sober lay preacher. Twenty-four hours earlier, he would be a brutal hit-man on the field of play. Derek Simpson was a 6ft 5in, 16-stone man-mountain who showed respect to his clubmates but little remorse or repentance after invariably barbarous contests with opponents.

He was a lock-forward with a take-no-prisoners reputation of being the hit-man, the assassin, the avenger.

Teak-tough on the field and a devout Christian off it, "Simmo" or "Simpo" believes his reputation has become exaggerated by the march of time.

"Yes, I think I got sent off about five times and received bans, but my reputation has got distorted over the years," he says now, at the age of 80.

One now-famous dismissal came at the start of a match in Wales between Swansea and Coventry.

Swansea had Welsh international Geoff Wheel in their ranks. Wheel had a pronounced facial tic.

Simpson was wound-up by his team-mates before kick-off. They told him: "If Wheel twitches, it means he's about to hit you."

Simpson believed the wind-up and recalls: "We were down in Swansea and Keith Fairbrother wound up the crowd and everyone else by doing a radio interview before the game and he said 'All Welshmen are bastards'.

"He then told me about this Welsh bloke's twitch. At an early line-out, he twitched at me so I hit him and put him down. The next thing I know, he gets up and starts hitting me.

"The ref came over and told Wheel to clear off the field and then said I should join him in the dressing rooms. We were still going for it as we left the field. I got on well with Geoff Wheel. He became a Christian later in life."

There is more than a hint of relish when he recounts his personal, very bruising battles on the rugby field. He joined Cov after leaving Coventry Welsh. He was a mature 29-year-old who had learned his craft at Burbages Lane under the coaching of Malcolm Lewis, who would eventually move to Nuneaton before becoming Coventry's coach.

"At Coventry Welsh, we had a player who we called Mr Magoo. I've forgotten his name. We were playing in the Welsh Valleys. Their team were all short and stocky and I had two of them trying to clobber me. I said to Mr Magoo 'Keep your head down at the next line-out.' He asked why and I said to just keep your head down.

"He didn't listen and at the next line-out I let go with a good bunch of fives and they had to carry Mr Magoo off."

Mr Magoo was actually hooker Jim McGuire, who wasn't the only Cov Welsh clubmate to be clobbered by Simmo.

David Hardy was a scrum-half destined to play for Coventry Extras and ultimately to become the Coventry club president in the year the Butts Park Arena was opened,

David recalls: "I can't remember who we were playing, but it was certainly the 1967-68 season and probably against a Welsh side.

"I was playing scrum-half and standing close to a maul waiting for the ball to emerge. There were a number of opponents lurking and waiting,

"Just as the ball became available, I was punched and ended up flat out on my back. The thing I remember was Simmo kneeling down and telling me how sorry he was, but he was going for an opposing wing-forward and missed."

But reunited with Malcolm Lewis at Cov, Simmo remembers a Thursday training session prior to a game against Moseley.

"Malcolm told the lads 'Our 14 are going to beat their 14.' We were puzzled and asked why 14? He said that I'd be marking a player called John Horton and that we'd both get sent off. It turned out to be true!"

On a social media banter page a couple of years ago, a Cov supporter asked where Simmo was these days. Back came the retort: "Not sure. I always assume in a corner somewhere chewing a brick!"

These days, he lives just a penalty kick from the Butts Park Arena and, like Bomber Evans, is suffering from Parkinson's Disease.

During his days as a passionate lay preacher, he spoke all over the country and he sang in a Barber Shop Quartet and revelled in a spiritual quartet with his wife and another couple.

"I was brought up a Christian and have been a member of the congregation in Spon End since I was a little boy," says Simmo, who was not the only religious man of the city to embrace the oval ball.

Across the city in Cheylesmore, was the Catholic priest, Monseigneur Tom Gavin, to this day the only man of the cloth to play for Ireland. Tom, who played for London Irish and Moseley, won two caps in 1949 playing with the fabled Jackie Kyle.

Coventry's Simmo never reached international status, though he was 'carded' as a non-travelling reserve. Still fiercely unrepentant of his on-field antics against opponents, he expresses regret at injuries suffered by team-mates during the heated helter-skelter of sporting combat.

"I would always stand up and support my team-mates," he said. "There were so many good talented lads coming through and Harry Walker told me to look after them. So I did.

"I remember a game down at London Welsh when a young Peter Preece got a blatant short-arm which laid him out. I ran down the field and decked the Welsh player. The tackle on Peter Preece was so blatant. Even the referee was aghast. He didn't even send me off!"

This all might give the totally wrong impression that Derek Simpson bent the rules, went over the top, and dished out brutal retribution from his 6ft 5in 'pulpit'. In truth, he was a fully committed rugby player, a hard man on the field, but a spiritual softie off it.

"After one game at London Scottish, one national newspaper the next day said something like 'Simpson practices a muscular Christianity'. I will not forget that."

And he would like to explode the myth that he was teetotal.

"I used to have a glass of red wine whenever I went to France, but I didn't drink with the lads. I just didn't like beer.

"The lads took advantage of that because I always ended up as chauffeur. It got me into trouble after one match. One of the lads had got married the previous day and we all went off to The Locarno after the game. He got hammered and I had to lift him into my car and take him home.

"I dragged him up the garden and knocked the door. The new wife of one day went berserk at me. She told me off saying things like 'How dare you get my husband drunk'. I ran back to my car, only to find he had been sick all over the back seat."

The doer of good deeds, the chauffeur, the avenger, the hit-man, the preacher, did actually find himself on the receiving end of a punch – from an unlikely source. It came, surprisingly, from match secretary Harry Walker.

"We had lost just a couple of games all season and we were playing Leicester in the final match," he recalled. "The perishers beat us. I was smiling as we came off the pitch. When I reached the dressing room door, I suddenly found myself on the floor. H had floored me.

"He said that when we win, we come off the field smiling, and when we lose, we come off the field crying!"

Divine retribution, perhaps?

Derek Simpson - the fearsome lay preacher

Photo: Emma Perry

Chapter Thirteen

Muncher and Cruncher: Two Iconic All-Rounders

S port will occasionally, fleetingly, toss together a time, a place and a man and allow all three to conjure a fabled unforgettable performance.

What Bannister did to the stop-watch; what Sobers did to Nash and what Matthews did to Bolton earned each a slice of immortality.

Those knights of the sporting realm occupy elevated status and Jim Stewart would squirm uneasily if anyone ever placed his achievement alongside theirs.

Still, the fact remains that generations of cricketers throughout the planet tried – and failed – to emulate his feat.

Big Jim spent his winters with Cov at Coundon Road and his summers with Warwickshire at Edgbaston. For this chapter only, I will christen him "Muncher" because Jim's renowned love of food had an impact on his burly frame. His appetite for big bits on the plate was only matched by his liking for bit hits on the playing field.

For decades, Wisden – the cricketer's bible – acknowledged Stewart's global record of 17 sixes in a match when scoring 155 and 125 for Warwickshire against Lancashire at Blackpool in 1960. Putting that into context, it meant he scored another "century" in the match – 102 in sixes alone! Remarkable. Astonishing.

A year after that effort, one of Coventry's greatest sporting sons was named on an MCC tour to New Zealand. An England cap beckoned. When he returned from the Antipodes to the Warwickshire fold, he bludgeoned 2,318 runs in the summer of '62.

The beefy ex-Broadstreet boy was on the verge – but the nagging pain that had plagued his left foot throughout the summer became intolerable.

Whatever ambitions Stewart harboured would be extinguished by a brutal medical term: amputation.

"I had to have my big toe off to save my foot," he said. "Gangrene had set in."

In his own words, he "struggled on" with Warwickshire for another eight years – but his chance of an England cap had gone.

Stewart had an unlikely introduction to cricket. Born and raised in the rugby hot-bed of Llanelli. He did not pick up a cricket bat until he moved to Coventry and attended Broadstreet School at the age of 12.

It was there that Harry Wapples ignited Stewart's burning passion for rugby football.

When I interviewed Stewart in 1986. he told me: "It was amazing how many quality rugby players Harry Wapples produced simply by playing touch-rugby in the school yard."

He went on to make 128 senior appearances as a centre for Cov.

His first three senior appearances for the club saw him mark, in turn, Alan Towell (Bedford & England), W.P.C. Davies (Harlequins & England) and Ronnie Burnett (Newport & Wales). It was a tough baptism.

"The last time I ever touched a rugby ball was when I played for Warwickshire in a County Championship final at Coundon Road."

That was in 1960 and Warwickshire beat Surrey 9-6. Ironically, Stewart won a championship title at rugby but, in nearly two decades, narrowly missed out on Warwickshire's glorious cricketing summers of 1951 and 1972.

At nearly 14 stone, Stewart was an overweight cricketer. "If I'd been a stone-and-a-half lighter, I'd have been a far better player, but I liked my food."

He rarely went to Edgbaston after he retired ("I am not a good watcher") but he retained links with Coundon Road.

He ran the Aubrey HIll sports outfitters in Coventry's City Arcade and it was Stewart who masterminded Cov's innovative sponsorship deal with Peugeot Talbot and it was he who provided Cov with their fabled blue-and-white jerseys.

After "Muncher" came "Cruncher" – John Gray, who easily slips into the category of Cov's best all-rounder.

If the world was oval-shaped and made of leather, Gray certainly picked it up and ran with it ... ending up halfway around the world.

Strongman Gray, Coventry's gift to Rugby League, always believed in grasping an opportunity with both hands. He went to Australia, where he became an icon and an idol

Indulging in the up-and-under Down Under gave him a lifestyle he could never have imagined when earning £14 a week as a teacher at Coventry's Binley Park School.

"On that money, I was never going to afford to buy a house for years," he said. "I went to Australia to give it my best shot. There's no point sitting back and wondering what would have happened if I hadn't taken the opportunity. When something like that comes up, you have to have a crack."

"If you've got talent, you have to make the best of it. I had talent but I didn't waste it because, let's face it, you're a has-been for a very long time."

Former England scrum-half and captain, Steve Smith, paid this glowing tribute to Gray in his autobiography. Wrote Smith: "Gray is one of the finest sportsmen to emerge from Coventry since the war. He is still the greatest all-round sportsman I have ever met."

Praise indeed. The ex-Woodlands schoolboy played soccer for Warwickshire Schools and had hardly played any rugby until he went to college. Within three years, he was Cov's first-choice hooker and had been on an England tour. He played cricket for the MCC Schools and was on Warwickshire's staff as a fast bowler,

Within 18 months of taking up a code-switching offer to take up Rugby League with Wigan, he was on the Great Britain tour to Australia.

Gray took it all in his stride. "There were some regrets at first," he recalled. "But they didn't last long. I missed Coventry and the lads at Coundon Road but the money was a big consolation."

He left Wigan in 1975 in a £14,000 transfer to North Sydney. In Australia, he made 198 appearances and scored 878 points. In 1976, he won the Amco Cup "superstar" prize after being named Player of the Competition.

He was one of the first players to use a round-the-corner place-kicking style. He was once offered £20,000 a year to kick goals in American "grid iron" football. That was a tidy sum in 1977. He turned it down, preferring the Aussie lifestyle instead.

"I only intended to stay in Australia for three years," said Gray. "But at the end of my contract, I had 10 clubs in for me offering so much money that I stayed on. I've been in Australia ever since."

Despite decades of Antipodean influence, there is no hint of an Aussie accent.

"No way," says Gray. "I don't like the way they speak. I'm a Coventry boy and I will always be a Coventry boy. I'm proud of my city."

John 'Cruncher' Gray ... a brilliant all-rounder

Jim Stewart: A brilliant all-rounder both with the willow and the oval ball

Photo: Tony Dickinson

Chapter Fourteen

A Presidential Salute to Coventry & England's John Barton

I t was going to be a joy, a chance to reminisce, a time to natter about days gone by. But it never happened. Fate intervened. His email said: "Call me anytime. I'd be happy to chat. Here's my 'phone number...."

I knew he was ill, but not that ill. By the time I got around to calling, he had just been discharged from hospital and nurses were upstairs in his bedroom which was adorned with Coventry and England memorabilia. The nurses were in awe of a brave battler.

John Barton was dying. My 'phone call came too late for him to add his cherished memories to this book. We lost him on January 12th 2021.

A few days after his death, his lovely wife, Mo, received a letter from Yorkshire. It summed up the brotherhood of the Rugby Football community. It was penned by a man who rose to great heights in the game and who just wanted to pay his respects and his tribute.

John Spencer won 14 England caps between 1969 and 1971. He was England captain in four matches. He was a British Lions tourist and later became manager. He went on to become President of the RFU and President of the Barbarians.

Hand-written tributes from someone of his pedigree and position are not lavished willy-nilly. And his admiration for the Coventry club – and John Barton – are huge.

In his letter to Mo, he wrote: "I hope you don't mind this intrusion from a rough Yorkshireman. I just felt that I wanted to contact you to express my respect for a good friend.

"I previously played for Headingley, Cambridge University and the Barbarians in many matches against Coventry when John was playing. We then played together in the England side and toured South Africa together in 1972 when we shared a room.

"At that time, most of the England side were from Coventry and so I felt privileged to make such good friends from the club. I am still in touch with David Duckham on a regular basis.

"John always welcomed me to Coventry and was always a gentleman in sport – except on the field! He was a talented ball-player and much respected on the international circuit. I always looked forward to seeing him in the E.R.I.C Room at Twickenham.

"Many old players have contacted me about John to express their sorrow. That is the rugby reality of our country's sporting heritage. There is a profound sense of friendship in our game and I hope you have experienced it in these difficult times.

"I will always remember John with a smile on my face. We enjoyed a few drinks together – particularly in South Africa. Off the field, he washed everything on the gentle cycle! He was a master at proving that friendship is the universal language of kindness.

"There are some people whose lives give themselves to memory, and John is one of them."

Lovely words Mr President. That letter sent salty streams cascading down the cheeks of Mo, who was also touched by a tribute appearing in the *ECHO*, the monthly community newspaper serving the Earlsdon, Chapelfields and Hearsall areas of Coventry.

Part of the obituary read: "John, who was 77, started his career with Caludon Castle Old Boys and made his name with Coventry as lock-forward from the 1961-62 season onwards, later moving to the No 8 position where he played in Coventry's first National Knock-Out trophy v Bristol in 1973.

"He retired in 1974/75, having played 265 times for Coventry, four times for England and also representing Warwickshire for whom he played in the losing County Championship final side in 1972 v Gloucestershire. He was also selected for the Barbarians and the Midlands regional teams.

"He won his England caps in the 1967 Five Nations tournament v Ireland, France and Wales (against whom he scored twice, a record for some years) and against France in 1972.

"At the time of his death John was due to be interviewed by former *Coventry Telegraph* journalist Steve Evans for a forthcoming book on the Coventry Rugby Club and sadly that will not happen, but his place in the pantheon of a golden era for Coventry is assured."

Proudly wearing his England tie: John Barton (1943-2021)

Photo: John Coles

Two Coventry and England line-out legends: Barry Ninnes and the late John Barton chatting at a Cowshed Lunch reunion

Photo: John Coles

Chapter Fifteen

Billy & 'Basil', Creed & Cowman: England Thoroughbreds

To be labelled a 'one-cap wonder' is mockingly cruel. To those who use the phrase, I would venture to counter: Better that, than be dubbed a 'no-cap wonder why?'

Coventry trio Bill Gittings, Barry Ninnes and Roger Creed each earned just a single England appearance. Each deserved more.

But I say 'tis better to have quenched the thirst for international recognition and sipped from Twickenham's fountain than to look back and lament what might have been, what could have been, but never was.

Thousands of envious players across the decades would happily exchange places with Gittings, Ninnes and Creed who each donned the fabled white jersey.

We lost the magnificent Bill Gittings a couple of years ago. He was living in America to be close to his precious daughters Nicola and Karen. The fact that Coventry Cathedral was bursting at the seams a few months later, as hundreds turned up to pay their respects at his memorial service, was testimony to his legacy and his popularity.

Coventry clubmate and president, Peter Rossborough, paid tribute. He said: "He had an infectious enthusiasm for life in general and rugby in particular. He loved the contact of the game, delighted in big hits in the tackle and smiling condescendingly at opposing players who tried it on with him. He was a pugnacious player with real guts and courage – a real Cov dog.

"He was a lovely man off the pitch, skilled and hard as nails on it. Bill epitomised Cov."

Daughter Nicola has named her son William in honour of her beloved dad. Bill Gittings, a proud product of Barkers' Butts, made 337 appearances for Cov and won his cherished England cap against the mighty New Zealand All Blacks in 1967.

Another so-called 'one-cap wonder' was wing-forward Roger Creed, who joined Cov from Solihull-based Old Silhillians, He dismisses the label by saying bluntly: "These days, a player can be sent onto the field for the last couple of minutes and not even touch the ball – yet he wins a cap. We earned ours for 80 minutes of hard graft."

He was one of Alf Wyman's recruits, recalling: "Alf kept asking me to turn out for the Nighthawks, the midweek team, and I stayed on. I was in awe of being in the same company as players like Phil Judd, Bert Godwin, Jim Broderick, John Owen, Harry Prosser, Billy Gittings, David Duckham, Sam Webb and Ricky Melville.

"There were no leagues in those days, so if you got a call to play for a club like Coventry, you dropped everything. Even your club was happy to let you go, because it was an honour. When I first joined Cov, they were all home-grown Coventry lads. Those of us from outside … well, they called us 'Brummie Bastards" in jest. It was a Coventry stronghold and to get invited to play, you had to prove yourself. I did, and I had some of the greatest times."

One of his most disappointing memories at Coundon Road was during his season as captain in 1970-71. "We got to the semi-final of the Knock-Out Cup against Gloucester. We drew 6-all and we came off the pitch thinking we had earned a replay. Then we discovered that Gloucester had won as the away side. Alf didn't know the rule. He was supposed to be our oracle."

Another match recalled, for different reasons, was a morning kick-off at Richmond. The Cov players were due to go to Twickenham in the afternoon for an England game. It was in the days before replacements and Cov had lost place-kicker George Cole to a bad shoulder injury and were down to 14 men.

Creed said: "We were losing, but scored a try in the last minute right in the corner. We needed to kick the conversion to win. George Cole was on the touchline with his arm in a sling, so we called him back on. George landed the kick and we won!"

If Roger Creed initially felt an 'outsider', moving just a few miles from Solihull, imagine how a 21-year-old Barry Ninnes coped with a move from his native Cornwall.

Barry, another who won just a single cap, became a stalwart lynch-pin of Coventry's second-row for more than a decade. To this day, much-loved, hugely respected.

Looking back on his decision to move "up country" from Cornwall to Coventry, he says: "Everyone back then wanted to play for Coventry. It was the best club in the land. These days, players just want to know who is going to pay the most."

He was another of Alf Wyman's recruits. "We had a chat and I thought why not give it a go, so I came up to Coventry as a 21-year-old and had a bed-sit off the Holyhead Road. One of my first training sessions, I was up against John Barton. He took the mickey out of me and called me a country yokel, but I partnered him and scored on my debut against Oxford. There were only two teams in Warwickshire as far as I was concerned – Coventry and Coventry Extras."

Like Creed, he is proud of his England cap and shrugs off the 'one-cap wonder' label with: "These days, they get five minutes as a sub and win a cap."

Recalling his England training camp and eventual call-up, he said: "I remember going down on the Thursday to Wales and, on the Friday, we all went for a cliff-top walk in Porthcawl, no tracksuits, just in our civvies."

All the squad was then called into a room and the selectors announced the team to face Wales the next day.

He said: "Rosie's (Peter Rossborough's) name was the first out of the bag as full-back and eventually my name was announced. It was a moment of absolute joy.

"Playing for Coventry was just as memorable. We had virtually an all-international back division and it was just phenomenal. I look back and one of the biggest highlights of my life was to take the field with some of the greatest players."

From Cornwall to Cumbria back in the amateur days, Coventry was a magnet. Workington-born Dick Cowman moved from just south of Hadrian's Wall to take up a teaching career in Godiva Land. He'd been studying at Loughborough when he saw a job opportunity posted on a university noticeboard.

His two subjects were chemistry and PE ... and there was a job going at Coventry's King Henry VIII School. He landed the position.

He would take the schoolboys to tournaments at Coundon Road and got involved with the club as a player. "It was amazing at Cov," said the England fly-half who won five caps. "With England, in just five Tests, I played with four different scrum-halves – Nigel Starmer-Smith, Steve Smith, Jacko Page and Jan Webster. In my entire career at Coventry, I only played with three – Grimshaw, Gittings and Gifford."

His last international was away against Ireland. "It was during the troubles and we had armed guards, but I have never heard such a roar from an opposing crowd as I did when we ran out onto the field. It was such a warm welcome. Our captain John Pullin said we may not have turned up and won, but at least we turned up."

Cowman, now living in Exeter, never played hard off the field while at Cov. He gave blood and sweat but declined the beers.

"I have never been drunk in my life," he insisted. "It has never appealed. The lads always respected me and joked that I'd probably get drunk on wine gums. I'd usually get a lift home before the fun started. There was one away game where the coach wasn't leaving until 11.30pm, so I went off to a local cinema to watch a film. When I got back, the lads were trying to haul a settee onto the coach!"

Cowman, who has four children, Chris, Tim, Jon and Beth, and 11 grandchildren, still insists on keeping fit by walking the Devon countryside. It is a slower pace these days, compared to taking part in the first Coventry Marathon and even enduring the London Marathon.

Looking back at his Coundon Road days, he says, simply: "I was just so amazingly lucky to be in the right place at the right time."

*****

To conclude this chapter, I would like to go back to Bill Gittings. Here, his daughters, Nicola and Karen, have penned a few words in tribute to their father – and have provided two fabulous images:

Being children of an avid rugby player comes with many highs and lows. Sacrifices obviously had to be made – the dedication to the team always came first. There were family celebrations that he always missed because he put his loyalty to whatever team he was playing for first but there was some good to be gained from that, both of us grew up to be very strong independent young women, with a strength and determination to be successful.

Dad's path to international rugby was not an easy one, his father passed away when he was just a teenager, he had to prove himself through his talent and love for the game, whilst taking care of his Mum and then a young family, rather than through influences that often lead to success.

We have many childhood memories of Dad playing rugby in the early days at Coundon Road, waiting by the tunnel for him to run out, smelling the liniment, the roar of the crowd on a Saturday afternoon, waiting with baited breath as Dad emerged from the bottom of a pile of players. He always managed to get us signed programmes from all the players, the laughter of the team and fans in the clubhouse after the games.

Those men and their families had a bond that has lasted a life time, we will be forever grateful for their love and support.

Dad would not have been the player he was without his strong resilient wife Anne by his side, being the wife of an international rugby player comes with many highs and lows too but she handled every situation with the same strength, grace and inevitably, a huge dose of humour. There were many Saturday nights spent at our house, with players leaving in the early hours of the morning. We are sure the neighbours didn't always appreciate it though.

Our Dad touched the lives of many people, which was very evident by the amount of people who attended Coventry Cathedral for the celebration of a life lived to the full. His love for rugby lasted until his dying days. One of the final games he watched was Ireland v England. He managed to sit up for half of the game and they were leading when he couldn't sit up any longer.

To everyone else he was a legend but to us his was "Our Dad".

The ambition: Bill Gittings (second row, third from the right), seated next captain Tony Gibbs, as a smiling schoolboy at Barkers; Butts School in 1953-54

Crowning glory: Just 13 years later, and former Barkers' Butts schoolboy Bill Gittings, head bowed, hand outstretched, greets his Queen before the England v New Zealand match in 1967. He is being introduced to Her Majesty by his Coventry and England captain Phil Judd.
(Both photographs courtesy of his daughters, Nicola and Karen)

Chapter Sixteen

Let's get ready to ... Basher!

L ike rutting stags, they locked antlers in constant tussles yielding blood, sweat and ultimate beers. Lee Johnson was an iconic member of the FRU. Nowt to do with the French. This is about the Front Row Union.

It was a fabled trio up front.

Johnson-Brain-Wilkes rolled off the tongue, the spearhead of a pack dubbed 'The Animal', claiming pushover tries with almost arrogant regularity.

Away from the scrum, Johnson was in his glorious predatory pomp, stamping immortality on a set-piece move known as *The Basher*.

He scored more tries than any other Coventry prop – 57, in fact, beating the previous record of 40 set by the late, much-lamented Jim Broderick.

One particular 'Basher' assumed almost Biblical status and will be etched in the memories of all who saw it at Coundon Road. It can only be described as The Parting of the (Welsh) Waves as Ebbw Vale were left awe-struck and AWOL as Johnson bashed his way to the line.

"Now I don't really know how the subtle move that is the Basher was invented and why I was the main practitioner," said Johnson. "But it became the perfect foil to the 5m pushover which yielded many tries for Godber (Graham Robbins) over the years."

The set-piece hinged on the immaculate timing and delivery of scrum-half Steve Thomas.

Said Johnson: "His timing was spot-on. His management of the would-be defenders was unbelievable."

Anyone who has ever shared the pitch with Tommo — team-mates, opposition and especially referees — will testify to his constant chatterbox approach.

"He made sure the ref made sure they didn't move early," said Johnson. "He would also warn the opposition to get out of the way because it might hurt!"

Johnson, who made 285 first XV appearances spanning 1975-1990, captained the club for two seasons in the mid-80s.

He came through the Coventry schools network and joined the club as a youngster. "A lot of would-be Cov players were plucked from this breeding ground by the legendary Harry Walker. Others would be reeled in by H's longer tentacles, a fair smattering of Brummies, the odd chap and even some from the far-flung corners of Britain and Ireland. To play for Cov was an honour and a privilege.

"To mix with internationals, divisional and County players was more than any young player could wish for."

Johnson gives an insight into classic post-match post-mortems with Harry Walker.

"Harry's love for, and knowledge of, the game meant performance analysis was short, to the point, and usually spot-on. No hours of video analysis, just a few chosen words.

"To hear Brainy and H exchange words was a joy. 'You old ......' was the prefix for every insult/expletive, rallies going on longer than any tennis match, each trying to make the last and worst jibe. None of it meant, but great entertainment."

Johnson's respect for Harry Walker runs deep.

"H was loved in Wales particularly and people would greet him like a long-lost brother and Harry would always respond with his best smile and a firm handshake.

"Steve Thomas would always ask 'Who's that H?'. Whilst Harry would often reel off the name of some bygone international, he would often reply: 'I haven't got a bloody clue'."

Harry was a prop-forward, like Johnson. but the latter-day prop evades comparisons between Then and Now, between Godwin-Judd-McLean and Johnson-Brain-Wilkes.

I will let proud Coventry kid 'Leebone' have his opinion.

"Cov has always had a traditionally strong pack. Not just big men. Not just men who could look after themselves. Not just men who could sort things out. A blend of all these. People who looked after each other – their own.

"The arrival of Steve Brain was the start of a long and memorable period when Johnson-Brain-Wilkes would ply their trade between 1981 and 1987.

"I think comparisons across the eras are difficult to make but I will settle for being mentioned in the same light as Judd-Godwin-McLean and Broderick-Gray-Fairbrother."

Johnson admits he was lucky to play alongside Steve Brain and Steve Wilkes but he pays tribute to those who were also called into front-row combat. He particularly points out lads like Martin Hobley, Max Reeves, Trevor Revan, Gareth Tregilgas, Andy Farrington, Roy Freemantle and Clive Davies "to name but a few."

Johnson has special affection for Wilkes and Brain.

He describes ex-Birmingham grammar schoolboy Wilkes, a schoolteacher, as "a Brum with a plum", but he points out: "He was an extremely caring and dedicated teacher in the Mr Chipps mould. On many occasions, he would mark books on the way to away games.

"He was no big drinker and rarely used inappropriate language. Wilksey got himself a motorbike. He famously, on the way to training in thick fog, decided it was best to follow the curb. Unfortunately, this led him into a lay-by and he hit the opposite side. Let's just say the lay-by won.

"Wilksey made it to training, scratched and cut, blood and gravel in equal proportions, and was met by a line of people offering to clean wounds with a scrubbing brush.

"For those to whom Wilksey inflicted wounds, mostly his own players, it was divine retribution. He was a fantastic scrummaging tight-head. Not the biggest, but technically and physically strong, but he was also the clumsiest bugger on earth. But we loved him."

Locking antlers alongside Steve Brain, destined to win England caps, was a joy. Brain went on to win caps against every major rugby nation within 12 months – a feat rarely achieved.

"He was fearless, tough and aggressive," said Johnson. "Brainy may not have been the quickest striker of the ball or the best thrower-in, but his presence was worth its weight in gold."

Whenever Brainy was late for training or challenged for claiming expenses, his stock phrase in his broad Brummie accent was: "Without a word of a lie ...."

Proud ex-Woodlands schoolboy Johnson found life in the front-row a bitter-sweet experience. He was an admirer of the non-stop chat of scrum-half Steve Thomas, directed at refs and oppositions alike. But he paid the price.

"Holding up that scrum sometimes meant donating layers of skin from my neck as layers of Vaseline became ineffective, knowing that Steve Beddis, our physio, had some spray-on antiseptic that he applied with his cheeky Scouse grin, taking pleasure in the stinging pain it delivered."

He could easily write an entire chapter on the "dark arts" of the front-row, like closing gaps to clash heads; binding illegally to get a better grip; or slipping the bind to attack the face of the opposing prop; or even "sending one through" from the second-row. Biting was rare, though it did happen.

Help from the second-row was part of the team effort and Johnson has special memories of lock-forward Derek Simpson.

"He was a religious man, a teetotal, and a lay-preacher with a reputation for sorting people out. It is amazing how crossing that white line impacts on people's behaviour."

It was a match against Gloucester United and Simpson, packing behind Johnson, kept asking "Are you alright?".

Johnson says he didn't need any 'intervention' but, at the next scrum, something happened.

"I felt this rush of air as Derek's fist flew past my right ear and right into my prop's face. The scrum broke up, the prop hit the ground. No more questions asked."

Those who reckon prop-forwards are thick, grunt-and-groan merchants should seriously reconsider. Steve Wilkes and Lee Johnson are two of the most articulate guys on this planet.

When I asked Leebone to contribute to this book, he mailed a response that would put Tolstoy's War and Peace in the shade. No journalistic exaggeration, but it stretched to a zillion words!

Devilishly, he headed it Let's Get Ready to Ramble and drew a smiley face and added "To be continued ...."

Six of the best: Lee Johnson (second from the right) with fellow front-rowers Thumper Dingley, Steve Brain, Harry Walker, Trevor Revan and Gareth Tregilgas.

Chapter Seventeen

Good Godber! What a No 8

He spent most of his career bending over and shoving his head in the vicinity of other blokes' backsides. And these days he answers his 'phone in the morning with the words: "Bore Da".

For a proud Brummie who won two caps for England, beating Wales on his debut, the fact that he is learning – and speaking – Welsh sums up his determination to blend in amid the foothills of Snowdonia.

Graham Robbins was No 8, the pack rudder, the tail-gunner – and, by jove, he certainly fired a few bullets on sporting pastures far and wide!

He scored more than 130 tries for Coventry, but was it 132, or 134, or even 136?

Not a bad tally for a forward, whatever the final total, the player affectionately nick-named 'Godber' cherishes his years at Coundon Road. His love for the club comes before any pride in statistics.

Why else would he risk his job, fake illness, to take time off work to play for his beloved Cov on a tour to Canada, scoring four tries under an assumed name?

Godber was working as an aviation fireman at Birmingham Airport in 1989 when the Canada tour was planned.

He threw a sickie and flew off, playing under the name of Dick Travers, just in case his renowned try-scoring exploits in North America made headlines back home.

He was a 20-year-old when he was recruited into the Cov fold by arguably the club's greatest latter-day talent spotter – Harry Walker, who was then match secretary of Coventry Extras.

"I'd played in the Warwickshire Cup for Sutton Coldfield against Stoke Old Boys, I think, and Harry and George Cole were watching the game," said Graham.

"I went out on the lash that night and, the next morning, my dad took a 'phone call from Harry asking if I would play for the Extras.

"I couldn't drive back then, so my mum drove me to the game and we picked up some others on the way – Andy Farrington, Steve Wilkes and Mercer Mottram"

He remembers that debut against Bristol United in the 1976-77 season because he met a "giant" by the name of Derek Simpson.

"He was bloody big," said Graham. "Paul Lander was getting a bit of stick from their lads and we got a penalty 10 metres out.

"Derek Simpson said 'We'll do The Puke'

"I'd never heard of it. It was my debut. Derek said just get on my shoulder and follow me. He went through their players like a bowling ball through skittles and I got my first try for the club."

The following season, he made his debut for the First XV. For him, it was awe-inspiring.

"I walked into the dressing room and there were players whose names I'd only seen in the *Rugby World* magazine. It was amazing.

"We started the season with games against the likes of Newport, Gloucester and Cardiff – remarkable when you think about it.

"I can't believe I was playing with guys like David Duckham, Geoff Evans, Peter Preece and Peter Rossborough and meeting someone like Peter Jackson off the field. I remember thinking bloody hell, that's the great Peter Jackson."

Looking back on his back-row partnerships, he speaks highly of flankers like Mel Parnell, John Shipsides, Mal Malik, Steve Oliver and, especially, his fellow Brummie Robin Sadler, describing him as "a real grafter."

But, of course, the iconic back-row trio was Dick Travers, Robbins and Paul "Mad Dog" Thomas.

"As a back-row, we went up against the best back-row combinations of Bath, Bristol and Gloucester and we absolutely annihilated them. We saw them picked for England and get a bit of recognition, but Dick and Paul were undersold and deserved the same England recognition."

Graham, who scored a try for the Midlands against the touring All Blacks and who was one of 15 Midlanders to become the only provincial side to beat the previously unbeaten, touring Australians, finally got his rewards.

"I got notification in late December that I was in line for an England call-up. I had to keep it quiet. I was at work at the airport and while my colleagues were concentrating on festive things, I was running up and down the bank outside the station carrying weights. I couldn't tell anyone."

But he helped beat the Welsh on his debut – something he doesn't really dwell on with his new neighbours in Cwm Penmachno, North Wales, where he is now captain of Betws-y-Coed Golf Club.

He remembers only too well how, when an English club was beaten heavily beyond Offa's Dyke, the locals would gloat along the lines of "Well boyo, you know that we only put out our third XV".

Said Graham: "All I've told them is that I played for Coventry and England, but they don't know that I scored against the All Blacks and beat the Wallabies."

Looking back on his 13 years at Coundon Road, he has so many fond memories – especially the Bermuda tour of 1980.

He particularly recalls an incident involving Dr Peter Brown, the club's doctor, who had fallen asleep on the outward-bound Jumbo jet.

"The lads asked one of the stewardesses for some make-up and lipstick," said Godber. "We did a great job on Doc Brown's face while he was kipping. He woke up and began chatting to Filbert Bayi (the Olympic runner who was bound for Mexico) unaware that his face was a picture.

"I remember Thumper Dingley disappearing to the toilet. He had shaved his beard and moustache off and came back wearing a wig. No-one recognised him.

"My times at Cov were the best times of my life."

Graham Robbins: Ready for action.

Majestic Cov

Chapter Eighteen

Steve Thomas: Schoolboy Captain Fantastic

J ust why Coventry's Steve Thomas missed out on a deserved full England cap remains one of the game's genuine mysteries. He was considered good enough to be named as captain of the England Schools 15-Group. He was still considered good enough to skipper the England Schools 19-Group.

But the next step, a graduation to the full England team, proved frustratingly elusive.

The former Coventry scrum-half looks back not in bewilderment or bafflement, but with a shrug of the shoulders and a frank acceptance.

"I would have loved a full England cap for sure, but it just wasn't meant to be," he says. "I had played for the Midlands in the Divisional Championship and we won the title.

"We were led to believe that it was a tournament to give options to the selectors, but they chose Nigel Melville and gave him the captaincy in 1984.

"I was chosen to sit on the bench for England for a match against the Barbarians but I didn't get on the field and, besides, no caps were awarded."

Coventry-born "Tommo" has always had a liking for the rough-and-tumble. Raised just off the London Road, his family moved to Rugby when he was 11 and Thomas candidly admits: "My parents decided to move to keep me out of trouble. I was always getting into fights with other lads."

He went to secondary school at Dunsmore where the rugby master was Wyn Morris, who was also coach to Rugby Lions.

"I was a soccer player, but I got introduced to rugby by Mr Morris. I was only just over 5ft 9in and I made my debut at the age of 11 in the second-row.

"By the age of 12, I had moved to No. 8 and then to wing-forward and eventually to scrum-half."

Astonishingly, he made his senior debut for Rugby Lions at just 15 years of age.

He spent four seasons at Webb Ellis Road before switching his allegiance to Coventry in 1979.

"I wish I had done it sooner, but I felt a loyalty to Rugby. They had been good to me."

Being the link-man between the forwards and the backs has taken its toll on the affable Thomas. The scrum-half in any team is invariably singled out by opponents. Thomas admits that he suffers from memory loss as a result of frequent head injuries sustained in the heat of battle.

"I think I got knocked out or concussed on at least a dozen occasions. And when I did a dive pass, a forward following through would often kick my head as I was laying on the ground."

He has been seeking help at a memory clinic but, so far, a condition known as Chronic Traumatic Encephalopathy (CTE), caused by frequent concussions, has been ruled out. So, too, has early onset dementia.

One brutal encounter at Coundon Road took place right in front of the Cowshed crowd.

"I can't remember who we were playing, but I threw a punch and missed," he said. "What I didn't know was that the player was an amateur boxer and he put me down."

Thomas staggered to his feet and his jellied heels betrayed his condition. Club physiotherapist Steve Beddis leaned him up against an advertising hoarding for a few minutes and "Tommo" boldly returned

Steve Thomas: Schoolboy Captain Fantastic

to the fray – only to collapse flat on his face. He took no further part in the game.

I vividly recall the day 'Tommo' ran out at Coundon Road to gasps from the Cowshed. He'd had his hair permed and I remember referring to him in the *Telegraph* as a Shirley Temple look-alike.

Looking back, he explained: "There was training twice a week, games every weekend and in midweek and I got fed up with having to sort my hair out after each session, so I had it permed. I took some stick at the time."

He looks back on his career – and the disappointment of not winning a full cap – and says: "We reached three John Player Cup semi-finals and lost the lot. Playing in a final at Twickenham would have been a showpiece for all the Cov lads to impress the England selectors, but we missed out."

After ending his playing career, Thomas was appointed as First XV Manager in 1992.

"I thought the world of those lads in the 90s. Coventry are a great club and I was honoured to play for them."

Is it Steve Thomas or Shirley Temple?
Cov's brilliant scrum-half, pictured after his hair-do make-over.

Chapter Nineteen

Simon Maisey: Cov's Answer to Forrest Gump?

Let's start by exploding the myth that when William Webb Ellis first picked up the ball and ran with it in 1823, he instantly passed it to Simon Maisey. True, Master Maisey was Head Boy at Rugby School, the game's birthplace, but that was in 1973, a mere 150 years later.

Mind you, running with the ball was instilled in him at an early age by his first rugby master Frank Drewett. He recalled: "As a 13 years old new boy at Rugby, having never played the game before and on a far flung exposed pitch on a freezing cold day, when I asked Mr Drewett what to do he said "catch the ball and run as fast as you can to the other end of the pitch". That was the best bit of coaching I ever had and is what I did every time I played."

That simple nugget of advice served him well during a Coventry playing career, which yielded 110 tries – gleefully one more than his good friend Peter Rossborough. In fact, there was something remarkable about his first team debut. Like an English version of Forrest Gump, he ran, ran, ran, ran and ran in five tries against Guys Hospital. What a baptism!

The magnificent game of rugby football has taken him on a memorable odyssey of our oval-shaped world. "I think back with a smile at all the many places the game has taken me in both this country and all over the world – Ireland, Australia, Canada, America, Caribbean, France, Italy, Netherlands, Chile and Argentina to name a few. Running out at The Arms Park or Lansdowne Road and at Twickenham with an England shirt on with my heart pounding and tears welling up singing the National Anthem. These are the happy memories and experiences that stay with me."

He earned England caps at Under-19 and Under-23 levels and other highlights include a hat-trick against the USA, winning the Heineken 7s against a Welsh international team in Amsterdam and winning the Quebec 7s in Canada. Sport throws up its slings and arrows and he admits to being in the Coventry team which lost 76-9 in Cardiff.

One of his biggest regrets is that he didn't fully apply himself to a game that would ultimately shape his life. "Regrets, I have a few but there again too few to mention" is how the song goes. It is how I feel when I look back. I should have trained harder and tried harder to see how far I could have gone. "Having said that, I would not change anything and I will be eternally grateful to the game and Cov for giving me so many happy memories and for making so many friendships.

"There are three people, whose kindness helped to make the player I was – Frank Drewett, who taught me how to tackle strongly, field an up and under kick and get properly fit for the England Schools' trials; Bill Martin, who transported me out of school on many a Sunday to play for Kenilworth Colts, which got me into the county schools team; 'H' Harry Walker, who pestered me after I left school to return home from working in London and to leave Rosslyn Park. Consequently, as a thank you, it was such a pleasure to organise his last three birthday parties at the Cowshed Lunch, celebrating his 103rd birthday at the last one. If all those calls and messages from Keresley 4842 had not been left for me, who knows where my rugby life would have taken me?

"Running fast and avoiding tacklers came easily to me and so when by chance I bought a house next door to David Duckham in Kenilworth, we used to do some summertime sprint training together up the hills in the Abbey Fields. How many young wingers get to be friends with and live next door to someone as famous and brilliant as Quackers? We still remain firm friends."

As a boy, he was sent to Coventry Preparatory School and then became a boarder at Rugby School. In some ways, it was a sheltered life. He didn't, for example, read copies of the *Coventry Evening Telegraph*, nor did he know about the exploits of the legendary

Coventry and British Lions winger Peter Jackson. "I didn't realise, when I joined Cov, just how famous and what a brilliant player Peter Jackson had been. He regularly attended mid week training and I missed the chance to ask him for advice and help.

"As a young player, I relished playing in a back division of full internationals, with me being the odd one out! In that period, before most games there was a feeling in the changing room that we were going to win and just the matter of by how many points – confidence oozing from the pores of every player. Then there were the nerves before playing Cardiff at a packed Coundon Road and the likes of stars like Gareth and Barry. Trips to Wales facing JJ, Gerald, JPR, Clive and Phil (you don't need the surnames even now)!

"So many memories of great craic – drinking in Dublin on a Friday night with Wanderers' players, only to find on Saturday afternoon they were the 2nd team and the 1st team had been tucked up in bed; my first away game for the club in the Extras at Roundhay, and until late into the night, playing drinking games with Brodders (Jim Broderick) the judge and Pumpsie (Paul Bryan) chief spy, with neat gin as the punishment. Tours to play Bezier, who had been French champions for 10 out of the previous 11 years and the coach to the game taking us en route through a nudist colony, and to Venice to play Treviso, with the well told story of Fazza (Andy Farrington) jumping off an upper floor hotel balcony and falling through an awning. I could go on."

In his early days at Cov, he would drive from London to play for the club, making almost every game an away match. They were tough times, especially during the three-day week and the miners' strike. "There was a Cov supporter with a garage en route, who supplied me with petrol so I could travel back to London. We met every Sunday night at 8.00 pm to fill up my tank. I did play for Rosslyn Park for a while until the regular phone calls from 'H' finally persuaded me to see the light and switch to Cov."

Simon remains a committed clubman, determined to put something back into a club that has consumed him and shaped him. He has a vast database of contact details for former players and, every February, he rallies them for the annual Cowshed Lunch – a gathering of chaps, who share a special bond of brotherhood.

Simon Maisey scoring one of his 110 tries for Cov,
with Graham Robbins in support

103

Simon Maisey in full flow with Colin Grimshaw in support.

*Ready to fill jugs with ale ... Simon Maisey in his role as
organiser of the annual Cowshed Lunch*

Chapter Twenty

The Red Rose Resurrection

Stars descended on Coundon Road and illuminated a cherished pasture like never before in the early 70s. They were not celestial, tumbling from the Heavens. They were human, home-grown, each destined to have a typographical star after his name – a humble asterisk denoting international stardom and twinkling terrestrial talent bearing the hallmark MADE IN COVENTRY.

Barren years followed but, then in the early 80s, there was a Red Rose Resurrection, a renaissance, a re-birth of a club's renewed affinity with the Twickenham selectors.

Like eager fishermen, the chaps from HQ cast their nets once again in the direction of Coventry and their haul yielded a quality catch – a quartet of Graham Robbins*, Huw Davies*, Steve Brain* and a player with an appropriate surname, Marcus Rose*.

I deliberately adorn each name with the asterisk that was destined to follow them whenever their name appeared in club match programmes around the country.

Between them, they swapped the blue-and-white hoops of Coventry for the dazzling, rose-adorned white of their country.

For two of them, their international lift-off would involve airports.

When he got his call-up, Graham Robbins virtually had to sign the RFU's Official Secrets Act. And his clandestine antics almost got him arrested!

The player affectionately dubbed 'Godber' might easily have served his own Porridge time.

Sworn to secrecy about his elevation from Cov to the national team, while serving as an aviation firefighter at Birmingham Airport, he unwittingly attracted the attention of the police.

During his evening shift break, he left the fire station and went jogging up and down the grassy, muddy embankment skirting the airport perimeter.

There was a high terrorism alert at the time, and the shadowy, twilight figure legging it around the airport, as if on the run, soon caught the attention of the boys in blue. They gave chase. Armed? Who knows?

Suffice to say, Godber was collared. The breathless, mud-spattered copper yelled: "STOP! What are you doing?"

Recalled Robbins: "I told him I was in training, but couldn't tell him why. The poor chap was covered in mud chasing after me, so I took him back to the fire station to get him cleaned up. I'm sure he thought I was a phantom terrorist. But everything turned out OK.

"When I got my call-up, it felt like I'd been named in the New Year's Honours list but couldn't tell anyone."

If Godber was spared a stretch of Porridge, Steve Brain's airport experience very nearly ended his England career before it had even got off the ground.

Selected to make his debut in South Africa against the Springboks in 1984, he missed his internal flight from Port Elizabeth – not once, but twice.

It put his debut in peril. Like Robbins, he was ordered to remain silent and not discuss anything with the touring Press Pack, eager for back-page scandal.

All these years later, the truth can be told.

Brainy revealed: "I had a good mate living in South Africa. I'd worked with him as a brickie. Though he was Welsh, he was a Brummie lad like me and he came to our hotel and got on with all the lads and even the hierarchy. He was a really sociable bloke.

"He asked me if I fancied having dinner with him and his family outside Capetown even though we were due to fly the next morning. I was told to be back in time. We enjoyed the dinner and I even got up to toast the Queen.

"Anyway, we set off for the airport, but his car had a puncture and I missed my plane. I spent the night at his place and we got absolutely steaming. I fell asleep on the sofa."

So he missed his second flight.

When he finally rejoined the England party after another hastily-arranged flight, he faced the outrage of the RFU hierarchy.

"I was given a right bollocking and they said they were debating whether to send me home in disgrace. They sent me to my room and said I should not talk to anyone."

As it turned out, he was forgiven and he went on to win the first of his 13 caps. Because of a fixture list quirk, he actually played against every major nation in the world in the quickest time.

One of the sport's real characters, granite hard yet affable, he looks back on his days with Cov as the best of his career.

You might think that running out at Twickenham, Johannesburg, Cardiff, Edinburgh, Dublin or Paris would fill a player with huge pride. True, but Steve Brain insists on pointing out that his biggest thrill was running out at Coundon Road.

"It was just the most uplifting atmosphere," he said. "When the game approached, I used to have butterflies thinking about running out to be greeted by the Cowshed. The atmosphere at Coundon Road was amazing. You couldn't bottle anything like that."

Both Robbins and Brain have memories of the late Ken Pattinson, the North Midlands Society referee and ex-player who went on to take charge of internationals. And both memories revolve around Cov scrum-half Steve Thomas.

Pattinson was in charge of a midweek match between Cov and Nottingham at Coundon Road. Opposing hookers Brain and Brian Moore were sent off.

"He (Moore) had just flattened Tommo, so I went for him," said Brain, always a player to stand up for his team-mates and dish out retribution. "We were both on the floor and I felt this arm trying to pull me off, so I elbowed him. It was the ref's arm and we both got sent off."

Steve Thomas was a brilliant scrum-half renowned for his constant natter on the field. He didn't pull any verbal punches and hit opponents and referees alike with equal insults.

Pattinson was refereeing another Cov game and Robbins recalls an exchange of expletive-loaded banter between Tommo and the ref.

Said Robbins: "The ref awarded a penalty against us and Tommo let rip along the lines of 'Ref, you're a bleep bleep.

"Ken Pattinson marched him back and said 'You may think I'm a bleep bleep, but you can't call me it. Quick as a flash, Tommo replied 'Well, I THINK you're a bleep bleep. All the lads were in hysterics."

Tommo escaped punishment because Pattinson, bless him, was an ex-player who knew and appreciated the on-field banter.

Robbins goes as far as to say that Steve Thomas – an England schoolboy international and captain – should have gone on to win full England honours.

"Tommo was easily the best scrum-half I have ever played with or against," said Robbins. "Even as a neutral, I rated him the best in the land. He should have won full caps."

I remember going down to Twickenham on a snowy December day to cover the 100th Varsity Match. It was special for the Coventry club because there were three Cov players on view. Chris Millerchip (Oxford University full-back) and Huw Davies (Cambridge University fly-half) and Marcus Rose (Cambridge University full-back). For a club like Cov to boast both full-backs was unheard of in the club's history.

Marcus Rose and Huw Davies were imports who graced Coundon Road fleetingly and then moved on.

It was the dawn of the professional era and gifted players were much sought-after. Cov, in all honesty, just did not have the funds to compete.

Ultimately, Rose went to Harlequins and Davies went to Wasps but the Red Rose Resurrection at Coundon Road was destined to enter barren times as the decade unfolded and the £ became an ever-attractive lure.

Players like Darren Garforth, Danny Grewcock, Richard Cockrell, Graham Rowntree, Neil Back and Dean Richards – all home-grown in the Coventry and Warwickshire fold – all sought fame elsewhere.

Coventry's purse strings simply could not compete nor keep pace with the rapidly advancing professional dawn.

Mates forever: Marcus Rose and Huw Davies at Coventry's Cowshed Lunch in 2018. Both were capped while playing for Cov.

Huw scored a fabulous try in an 11-10 Coventry defeat at Maesteg ... but few people were aware of what that try meant to him.

His grandfather, Emlyn, was a pacey winger for Maesteg in the 1920s. He moved to Bridgend just down the valley and was approached by Cardiff, where a certain Welsh cap beckoned, but it was too far for a valley boy miner to travel. Huw's father, Vernon, also played for Maesteg as a centre. So, three generations of Davies boys graced the turf at the Old Parish ground over a 60-year period.

Photo: Alan Joseph

Chapter Twenty-One

Like Father, like Son?

This chapter is devoted to proud sporting dynasties ... sons who followed their dads and pulled on the fabled blue-and-white of Coventry.

A sk a player known as Mad Dog why he embraced rugby and the answer comes quicker than Erica Roe could bare her boobs at Twickers.

"It was the legalised violence," chuckled Paul Thomas, as fast as a flasher – a lightning response which probably explains how he got his nickname.

Tommo yearned for the rough-and-tumble of the oval ball rather than court the other code so passionately embraced by his father and two brothers – all three of them, professional soccer players. But more of this later.

Now ask a player nicknamed The Pig why he chose rugby despite his dad being a Coventry City FC legend.

Mick Curtis says simply: "Because you could almost get away with murder and share a beer with your opponent after the game."

His dad, George 'Iron Man' Curtis, made nearly 500 appearances for the Sky Blues and, with John Sillett, masterminded the club's finest hour – the FA Cup triumph at Wembley in 1987.

"I was just a kid," says Mick, who made more than 200 appearances for Cov spanning a dozen years. "Dad was really busy at Highfield Road and I used to go and sometimes I'd end up being the mascot."

At Woodlands School, he played soccer. He was a centre-half, just like dad. "I really used to tackle hard from behind, but then they tightened the rules and so I switched to rugby and joined Trinity Guild."

He joined Cov, where the son of the Iron Man was christened The Pig (he even has a bar in his back garden called The Pig Inn) because of his love for bacon sarnies.

Voted by the supporters as Player of the Year in 2003, he retains huge respect and regard for the fans, the club and his birthplace city.

"One thing about the Coventry supporters, whether you had a good game or a crap game, the Cowshed would always let you know and buy you a beer afterwards. I have massive passion for the club and the city. If they do eventually expand the Butts Park Arena, I hope they put in a new Cowshed. The banter from the crowd is wonderful."

The Curtis sporting dynasty does not end with Mick. There is his son, George Jnr, now 23 and on the verge of following in his dad's bootsteps with Cov. As a kid, he was a ball-boy at Coundon Road. His mum, Marti, recalled: "He was only a little boy, but he once led the team out onto the field and he even wanted to join in the huddle before kick-off!"

A modest, versatile back who has played for England Colleges, his progress has been stumped by lockdown but he harbours ambitions. After all, The Piglet carries the magnificent Curtis genes. Watch this space.

But, now back to Paul 'Mad Dog' Thomas who, like Curtis, abandoned the family soccer tradition. Paul's dad, Barry, born from Welsh stock and christened Brynley, was a centre-forward on Coventry City's books in the 50s. Paul's brother Dean played for Wimbledon, Fortuna Dusseldorf, Northampton, Notts County, Bedworth and was Hinckley United's manager for a record 15 years. His brother Wayne played in Germany and succeeded where Kevin Keegan failed – by winning a German FA Cup-winners medal.

Paul has already spontaneously answered why he took up rugby instead of soccer and he says: "I think dad was quite pleased because his father was a Welshman and he loved rugby. I was playing soccer at Ash Green School but one of my pals, Steve Hancox, was turning out for Coventry Saracens and I caught the bus to Kirby Corner and turned up."

He ended up at Cov and looks back on his career at Coundon Road in the back-row with pride. There are no regrets about turning his back on soccer. He puts it like this: "When you come from a sporting family and they throw you a ball, you can play with it and run with it. I wanted to run with it, not kick it."

Harry Walker and Ivor Preece are easily two of the most iconic names in Coventry's history – and proud dads, too.

Ivor's son, Peter Preece, went on to win the same number of England caps as his dad.

Peter said: "He always encouraged me, but never pressured me. At King Henry VIII School, it was wonderful to be playing with lads like David Duckham and Peter Rossborough."

His 'debut' at Coundon Road, if you can call it that, was not actually on the field of play.

He recalls, with a smile: "My introduction to the ground was as a child and I used to watch the games but also help look after the scoreboard in the corner on match days, putting the metal numbers on the board whenever there was a score."

Harry Walker's son, Richard, was just like dad, hard as nails. 'H' won England caps either side of the war and ran pubs around the city – the Old Hall in Lythalls Lane; The Grapes in Radford and the Golden Eagle, off the Foleshill Road.

Richard recalls: "Because 'H' was a pub landlord and a well-known rugby player, all the players used to pile back to the pubs he ran. I grew up around rugby players."

Richard, a Bablake boy, was encouraged by his dad to play rugby. "He'd send me up as a kid to play for Dunlop thirds. I was hooking with all these hairy-arsed blokes."

He went to Newcastle University and ended up playing for Gosforth. His father was a well-known name but Richard kept quiet. "I didn't tell anyone he was my dad because it might have made me a target. In one match for Gosforth, there was an injury and I was put on the wing. I scored two tries. I thought I'd be bloody stuck out there on the wing.

"Eventually, I came back to Coventry and played for the Extras as a wing-forward. Rugby was in my blood but 'H' was never one to tell you what you did right. He would only tell you what you did wrong. Not just me. All the players. I looked up to him."

A more recent father-son contribution to Cov came in the shape of two big lads – Tony Gulliver and his son, Ben.

Former lock-forward Tony, now the team manager, remains one of the club's long-term faithful servants. Ben has massive respect for him.

His professional career has embraced Ampthill, Coventry, Saracens, Plymouth Albion, Cornish Pirates, Leicester, Worcester Warriors and Bedford – a terrific tumbleweed journey which started as a baby cradled in his mother's arms while she yelled "Come on Gully" from the Coundon Road stand.

Supporting Cov was always a family thing. It became a ritual, a regular jaunt on Gulliver's Travels.

Said Ben: "My grandfather and grandmother used to take me to away games to watch my dad play. My early memories of Cov are full of grandma and grandad. They were lovely. I always think back and say that those days were the forgotten era. The players of those days were my heroes."

But there was one hero who stood taller than all the others – his father, Tony. "Yes – he was my real hero. My goal number one was to one day play for Cov just like dad. It was a positive journey."

After escaping from his doting mother's lap as a baby, he was eventually unleashed to run free on the pitch perimeter where he became an astute ball-boy.

"I would always give Cov a clean ball, but if it was the opposition, I'd give them a muddy, mucky ball."

One of his early memories is of Steve Thomas giving up his post-match drinking time to take him out onto the field to teach him kicking skills. It was to be the launch of a friendship that would span the generations and endure to this day. He was holidaying in Ibiza with his good lady Georgie (37 caps for England Women) when he heard a familiar voice say: "Hello Gully." It was Steve Thomas's son, who was working out there. Small world.

Ben retains huge respect and admiration for his dad. "I don't think I have ever met a man who loves Coventry so much. He lives and breathes for the club. He is my inspiration."

Ben's last game for Coventry was against Canada – a match heavy with emotion. Only a few months earlier, former Coventry and Canadian international centre John Cannon had died from a heart attack at the indecently young age of 35.

"John was one of a kind – a true friend," said Ben. "I flew to Canada and was one of the pall-bearers at his funeral. It was fitting that my last game for Cov was against Canada."

And now we come to a happy ending – a father and son who actually played together.

Glyn Owen was a utility back with Coventry between 1985 and 1989. A half-back by nature, he made his debut on a freezing day at Fylde, standing in on the wing after Eddie Saunders somehow got lost in the Blackpool suburbs. He actually scored a try to crown his debut.

Eventually, Glyn returned to the Kenilworth club and had the proud honour of being on the field when his son, Will, ran out to make his debut at the age of 17.

Will, who is now on Coventry's books, recalls: "I remember that match against Earlsdon because my dad landed the winning kick.

"I remember going to watch dad at Cov. I used to stand in the Cowshed as a kid. It inspired me. It planted a seed in my mind that, one day, I would love to join the club."

And so he did ... a lad, like those before him, who followed in his father's bootsteps.

Like Father, like Son?

THE HOMECOMING
England captain Ivor Preece, after six months away with the British Lions, returns to greet his baby son Peter – destined also to play for Coventry and England.

Former Coventry City player Barry Thomas with his sons Dean, Paul and Wayne

The Walker family - Harry, Richard, Ross and young Tom

Photo: Simon Maisey

Icons of Coventry Football Club (RU) ...Tony Gulliver with his son Ben.

Mick Curtis with his dad George, a Coventry City legend.

Father and son: Glyn and Will Owen

Chapter Twenty-Two

Wearing a Cov Tie to Help Restore the Entente Cordiale

It was just a tie, a humble blue and white tie, but it caught my eye. Through the haze of Gauloise cigarette smoke in a French bar while the locals were savouring the joie de vivre of beating the English, I saw that tie.

I recognised it. Not any old tie. It was being proudly worn by a bloke who said he was from Bristol. But it was a Coventry tie. So I quizzed him. He introduced himself as Bob Frame. He was George Cole's half-back partner at Coundon Road back in the day.

He was a stranger to me before I clocked the tie, but it was though I had known him for ages. We shared a few guzzles and went our separate ways on the day that the oval-ball guys restored our nation's faith in cross-channel sportsmanship.

Jon Sharp was there that day, but I didn't get to bump into him, a massive Cov fan who some would describe as a supporter who became a saviour.

Anyway, back to the day. We had earlier walked the sinister gauntlet of a thousand batons, automatic weapons, and we quietly set about polishing England's tarnished sporting reputation.

We succeeded admirably, but then none of us really had any doubt.

This was, after all, a rugby trip and, as anyone knows, the boys in tweed caps are a different breed.

Thousands of us, including the boisterous but good humoured lads of Coventry, Stoke Old Boys, Broadstreet, Trinity Guild, Kenilworth and Leamington were making not so much a sporting pilgrimage but a mercy mission.

Mercy, we were warned, was something we could not expect from the feared French CRS riot squad who seemed to fringe every boulevard leading to the swank concrete ampitheatre that is the Parc des Princes.

But, merci beaucoup, we got it. They eyed us up, unsmiling and wary, with the words of Jacques Chirac, the Mayor of Paris, ringing in their ears: "Tan the hide of the English," he had barked, in the event of any trouble.

In the shameful aftermath of the English soccer rowdies at the same venue, here we were, just three days later, facing the possible backlash of French antagonism.

We were there to pick up the tab; to restore Anglo-French relations arguably at their lowest ebb since Agincourt. And we did it.

One French newspaper carried a page 3 picture across five columns showing a group of English fans draped in the Union Flag that had been so badly let down by the followers of the round-ball game. One of the lads had turned away from the camera to reveal a placard on his back. It was decorated with a red rose and a rugby ball and it said "SVP - Ne nous confondez pas avec des supporters de football".

Roughly translated, the young man was begging not to be confused with the soccer rabble. He got his message across. It went down well with our hosts.

Even so, we still had to walk that gauntlet after mixing amicably with the French in the bars and cafes and raising deep red glasses in expectation of a new entente cordiale.

The thick, blue lines of CRS men had set up checkpoints every hundred yards or so with dozens of cold grey battle wagons, each with intimidating barred windows, parked nearby. Surely it's easier getting across the Russian border?

Tickets checked. Again and again. Cautious glances mutually exchanged. Serious scrutiny and then: "Ok merci" – or was it mercy?

The guns stayed holstered and rifles remained on shoulders and, once inside the ground, there was the joyous relief of klaxons and live cockerels.

The Clochemerle bands in the crowd offered spontaneous entertainment at every lull in the action and "Allez, allez France" was answered by "England, England, England". It was good-natured and good-humoured and we smiled at the programme misprint which had Nick Stringer, one of the England replacements, as STINGER (Wasps).

I got nattering to a French photographer after the game and, in his pidgin English, got his message across about the English rugby fans.

"Zay are not ze animal like soccer."

As we left the ground, the CRS were still out in force but redundant.

So deliciously redundant. Then, shoulder to shoulder with our French counterparts, we allezed to the Metro and then on to the bars around the Boulevard de Clichy to toast not so much a defeat on the field but a success off it.

And to reflect sadly on the gauntlet that had been thrust upon us by those who follow the other code.

There will never be a military-style operation mounted at Twickenham, or the Arms Park or Lansdowne Road or Murrayfield, but will Paris ever be the same again?

It will because of dapper chaps like the late Bob Frame, suited and booted and proudly wearing his Coventry tie.

Cross-legged but never a cross word between them: Fly-half Bob Frame is flanked by two iconic scrum-halves – George Cole (left) and Bill Gittings.

Chapter Twenty-Three

Farewell to Coundon Road

They turned out in force to say a fond farewell to a fabled acre, a field of dreams, a stage upon which the game's immortals hugged the leather and danced.

On the terraces, beneath the rusty, ramshackle roof of a vantage point known dearly and devoutly as The Cowshed, they looked down on the springtime greenery for one last time and they lamented the end of an era.

It was the day legions of Coventry kids stood together in one last taste of Coundon Road camaraderie, one final boisterous bellowing of banter from the 'Shed', and one ultimate act of remembrance.

It was the day they gathered on the outskirts of a cathedral city to say goodbye to a sporting shrine long regarded as a High Church of the oval-ball code.

It was akin to Leicester taking their final bow at Welford Road, or Gloucester at Kingsholm, or Northampton at Franklins Gardens, or even Manchester United at Old Trafford or Warwickshire at Edgbaston.

It was difficult for the fans to concentrate solely on the match unfolding before them because, on occasions like that, the mind keeps flashing back to the ghosts and the echoes of yesteryear, when Cov were arguably the greatest club in the land and giants trod the turf.

Anyone who has ever made the pilgrimage to the old cabbage green stands of Twickenham for, say, a game against the French will know what I mean.

A date with the French was always a colourful assault on the senses – Gallic sounds, garlic smells and grand sights, klaxons, cockerels and Tricolours, a blazing honking unmistakable French Armada.

HQ was where you shared a beer with Jacques or Jock, Dai or Dermot, depending on the nationality of that day's invasion of London suburbia.

It was the same at Coundon Road, though not nearly as grand of course, when thousands of Cornishmen filled the ground in the 60s for classic County Championship encounters, or when once-mighty Cardiff were regular visitors and every flat-capped miner called Williams or Davies emerged from the Warwickshire coalfield to declare their allegiance to their classy counterparts from beyond Offa's Dyke.

I have always regarded the Cowshed as a little cousin of the Anfield Kop and the spiritual home of some of Coventry's most knowledgeable followers. The humour has always been ribald and risqué, but they know a good player when they see one and, over the years, they have seen a glut of good players.

The Honours Board is a testimony to that and a tribute in a manufacturing city to the awesome production line of Coventry Football Club (RU).

Etched in gold letters are dozens of names of international players who have now passed into Coventry folklore – each one revered because he wore THE jersey with a woven red rose across the heart.

That proud emblem of English rugby achievement, sewn on dazzling white, bloomed more than ever at Coundon Road during the early 70s.

Some, like the dashing David Duckham, were handed what amounted to bouquets. Others, like Bill Gittings and Barry Ninnes, were given a derisory but no less cherished single stem.

Back in 1973, England beat the fearsome All Blacks in their own back yard for the first time. There were five Coventry lads in the team that day.

It boiled down to this: a little field of dreams in the very heart of England had honed the skills of a quality quintet destined to humble a team who were then regarded as invincible.

There was an air of solemnity about the curtain falling upon Coundon Road, a sense of bereavement, a gut-wrenching feeling that you were burying an old pal.

It was not the end of an era. It was merely the end of a chapter in a city's proud sporting chronicle.

Stalwart supporter Barrie Duckett supplied this image of friends gathered in front of the Honours Board on Coundon Road's final day. He also penned these words:

The 17th April 2004 is a day that will live long in the memories of many of the Cov faithful ... the last ever game at our beloved Coundon Road. On that beautiful Spring day the sun shone, the band played, the beers and the tears flowed and, before a crowd of 3,100, we beat the Manchester club 34-20 in a vital relegation battle. So that was that. The hallowed turf where P.B. Jackson jinked, George Cole toe poked goals by the thousand and D.J. Duckham frequently sent the Cowshed the wrong way with a searing sidestep was to become a housing estate but memories are kept alive with streets named after these club legends ... a nice touch. The ground may now be a distant memory but friendships formed there over the years carry on regardless. We no longer get rust in our beer from the Cowshed roof or slosh around on the beer soaked clubhouse floor (not to mention the gents at the back of the stand!) but that was all part of the match day experience. A cup of tea from the tea bar followed by a few pints, a chat with the players and the occasional sing-song in the crowded Pemberton Room ... these things may be gone but will not be forgotten by those who had the pleasure of experiencing them.

The fabled, much lamented "Cowshed" at Coundon Road.
Gone but never forgotten.

A sign which summed up Coventry's departure from Coundon Road
after more than 80 years

Chapter Twenty-Four

Trying Times on the Road

Travelling with the two "Jules" in Coventry's crown could be fraught with perils. I am not referring to Her Majesty's treasures but to Julian Hyde and Julian Horrobin.

Coventry City had their own gem of a man with the initials JH in the Sixties. Jimmy Hill took the Sky Blues on a fabulous promotion journey.

But, for the Cov JH duo, away days in the 80s and into the new millennium were littered with journeys that became comical jaunts.

Take Julian Hyde's trip to Nottingham, for example, being chauffeured by Coventry prop-forward Steve Wilkes.

Said Hyde: "He turned up to give me a lift in an old hand-painted Ford Cortina. We crawled up the motorway doing just 40 mph and there was a big hole in the floor about 10 inches in diameter. I saw so much of the M1 road surface on that trip. He got injured in the match and couldn't drive me back."

Another incident saw him forced into an unplanned game of Hyde-and-seek-out a lift after the team coach organised by Harry Walker broke down on the way to Leicester.

"I always enjoyed playing at Welford Road but that day we had real problems getting to the game. We flagged down a lorry and four of us got in the back with loads of welding equipment. The other lads all hitched lifts with supporters.

Harry Walker had a reputation for booking unreliable coaches, but more of that later in the chapter.

Hyde, nicknamed 'Donk' and 'Seal Pup' by his team-mates, played for Cov between 1987 and 1997 and was a formidable lock-forward. He left to join Birmingham Solihull, where he captained the club.

It was the dawn of the professional era and Hyde, a product of Barkers' Butts, said: "I didn't want to give up a good career at Jaguar Land Rover so I reluctantly left Cov."

His Coventry clubmate Julian Horrobin has painful memories of Hyde.

In his broad West Country accent, Horrobin said: "I'm sure he had corners on his body because he would split you accidentally. He was a menace – a real body-splitter."

Mind you, Horrobin was a brutal, take-no-prisoners tackler. In a game at West Hartlepool, he launched into a crunching tackle on the England and British Lions full-back Tim Stimpson.

"All I remember is hitting him with everything I had, but I knocked myself out and they had to use a pair of scissors to get my tongue out of my windpipe.

"Back in the changing room, I put my hand in my pocket but my wristwatch had disappeared. It had been nicked. The police turned up and interviewed me and I gave a statement. When I got home, I walked into my bedroom and, there on the side, was my watch. I'd been concussed."

Horrobin used to travel with his dad by car to matches and, just like Julian Hyde, he has memories of Leicester's Welford Road – not getting to the ground, but trying to get away from it.

"We had parked in a school car park near the ground, but when we got back, it had been locked up. The referee's car was also in there. We got put up for the night."

Which brings me to a now-legendary catalogue of transportation calamities.

An artist's palette could have summed it up by mixing the blue of the sky with Harry Walker's red face – because we were marooned.

Playing hop-scotch in a lay-by seemed an appropriately farcical alternative to playing rugby in the splendid Arms Park arena.

Marooned on an isolated Welsh road, after a comical catalogue of mechanical failures, Coventry's players passed the time in a way that summed up a journey that became a joke in September 1982.

By the time they reached their destination, the crowd's patience had long since evaporated and the Cardiff St Albans Silver Band had exhausted their repertoire.

The immaculate red-coated bandsmen had been booked for a 30-minute stint. Nearly three hours later, in temperatures soaring into the seventies, they were still out there on the pitch delivering their third rendition of a rather apt "All Through The Night."

It was the day that farce came to the Arms Park and tinged their national game.

For Coventry, setting out from Coundon Road at 10.30am, the welcome in the hillsides was less than sympathetic from a crowd irritated by a succession of broken promises about the amended kick-off time … 3.45pm … 4.15 … and finally 5.20.

Coventry's trip to the Principality started badly and grew steadily worse. They were initially delayed by holiday traffic and then refused access to the M5 by police because of a six-mile tail-back.

After a 15-mile detour, they crossed the Welsh border. Then, outside the market town of Usk, their team coach spluttered to a halt amid a cloud of blue smoke and steam. It was 1.50pm and, after an emergency call to the AA, a message was relayed to the Cardiff club who promised to send out a relief coach.

It never arrived. Apparently, that had broken down as well. The players made the best of it. Graham Robbins and Bob Massey played hop-scotch in the lay-by; Huw Davies read his 173rd page of Sherlock Holmes and Paul Knee risked ant bites reclining on the grass verge.

Meanwhile, back at the Arms Park, the public address system broke news of the latest set-back to a rapidly declining crowd. And the band played on.

Cardiff officials then dispatched a fleet of five cars to ferry the stranded Coventry players the 25 miles to the ground.

After more than two hours waiting at the roadside, rescue finally arrived and the convoy set off to complete the final leg of an ill-fated journey. Then came the sting in the tail.

The car being driven by Tony Williams, the Cardiff club chairman, blew its cylinder head gasket on the M4 and four of the Coventry party were marooned again. The convoy halted on the hard shoulder, and players were transferred to other cars.

But that still left Mr Williams and the Coventry match secretary Harry Walker without transport. They were forced to hitch-hike the remaining 10 miles to the Arms Park!

"I can't believe it," said Harry at the time. "It has been a disaster from the moment we left Coventry. Someone up there doesn't want us to reach Cardiff."

By the time Coventry arrived, the 6,000 crowd had dwindled to 2,000 die-hards.

Alan Priday, the Cardiff secretary, told me at the time: "I suppose you have to look on the funny side but we take our game very seriously down here and many in the crowd clearly lost patience with the whole sorry saga."

Before the teams finally kicked off – two-and-a-half hours late – the public address speakers boomed out: "The score at the moment is Coventry 1 broken down coach – Cardiff 1 broken down car."

It was fitting, then, that the match should end in a 25-all draw.

* A replacement coach was sent to South Wales to bring the party back and they arrived in Coventry at 3.25am on the Sunday morning – nearly 17 hours after setting off.

Contributions

The following chapters are tributes by some people who have been closely involved in Cov's history ... sports writers, players, and long-time supporters. They were all keen to contribute to this book with their own fond memories of the club.

Let's share these recollections ...

Chapter Twenty-Five

Walking with the Giants of Rugby

John Lamb

(Coventry Evening Telegraph former Assistant Editor)

I inherited the Cov bug from my mum. She would jump on the back of her brother Jack's motorcycle in the 1930s to follow the team home and away.

So, as I look back over my association with Coventry Football Club (the title never officially carried the word Rugby), I feel privileged to have been given the opportunity to have a close association with a club that for me is a world-wide institution that prevails even in these straitened times.

It was through my job on the *Coventry Evening Telegraph* in the late Sixties and Seventies that I was lucky enough to get to know members of a team that was at the zenith of its fame and popularity.

Here was a bunch of guys, all amateurs, from all walks of life who built one of the most feared club teams in the land. They were the best in England and, arguably, Wales.

I was privileged because, as a flanker of mostly second team standard for Keresley (a club of gentleman founded by my cousins John and Brian Goss), here I was mixing with some of the greatest players in the world.

Names like David Duckham, Keith Fairbrother, Peter Preece, Geoff Evans. Peter Rossborough, Alan Cowman, Barry Ninnes, Ron Jones, Sam Webb, Barrie Corless, John Gray, John Gallagher, Ian Darnell, Richard Walker, Colin Grimshaw, John Barton, Fran Cotton, Chris Wardlow and Bill Gittings regularly occupied the team sheet.

What a line-up and, of course, they inherited a pedigree created a few years earlier by the likes of Ivor Preece and Phil Judd, who would both go on to become England captains, and Peter Jackson.

I remember bumping into Phil in a Balsall Common newsagents shortly before he died. The guy behind the counter was astonished when I told him that the regular customer he had just served was a former England rugby captain. Phil's modesty was matched mainly by his skills and guiles as an uncompromising loose-head prop in that legendary Cov front row of Judd, Godwin and McLean.

In that very different age, hooker Bert Godwin was selected to go on a British Lions tour but had to turn it down because of work commitments.

As deputy sports editor at the *Telegraph*, rugby coverage was not my first responsibility but I was happy to deputise for Bob Phillips and then Michael Austin when they were away on holiday or covering representative and international matches.

And that meant on occasions travelling away with the team and I felt privileged at being allowed to travel on the coach with them.

Privileged but hardly comfortable. It seemed that the fleet of buses owned by Coventry president Tom Venn had all been stripped of their heating and I quickly learned, like most of the players, to ensure I had warm clothing with me for a return journey in the small hours of Sunday morning.

I recorded some of my experiences on away trips with Cov in my book *Telegraph People* (Takahe Publishing, £10.99), which is still available on Amazon and in book shops.

It was like travelling the country with the Manchester United of rugby. There was nearly always a huge crowd wherever Cov were playing, such was the charisma of a club boasting many England stars plus Welshman Ron Jones and Irishman Colin Grimshaw.

Not that their rugby was always sparkling and I remember one Cov forward telling me that they only gave the ball to the threequarters on the promise that they would quickly give it back to the pack. Quite right too, for Cov's fearsome eight was renowned the length and breadth of the country.

I wrote many match reports, comments and *PINK* pages on Cov for the *Telegraph* and later the *Birmingham Evening Mail*. But my first comment on their play was made from Coundon Road's Cowshed watching a mid-week Nighthawks match.

Ricky Melville was his immaculate self, playing on the wing right in front of the Cowshed aficionados. His hair was always immaculately groomed and held in place by Brylcreem, the pioneering hair styling product. When he dropped a high ball, I was moved to shout from the safety of the Cowshed: "What's up Rick, too much Brylcreem on your hands?"

Even when I left the Midlands for Fleet Street, my association with the club was maintained when my son James played in the back row for Coventry Colts.

This was part of a successful youth section for which I reluctantly agreed to become chairman. The real graft in creating a team comprising many promising players was carried out by Ian Carvell, John King, Ron Kempin (still devoting his time to the club as kit man) among many.

The club's fortunes have waxed and waned for many years since then. I always believe that had we not been blown away in the second leg of a play-off for a place in the top league by London Irish at Sunbury-on-Thames on a windy afternoon we would still be there today.

I'm full of admiration for Jon Sharp, who has pumped huge amounts of money into the club to keep it afloat. And he follows a long line of people who dedicated much time and energy into keeping a great club at the top.

It was a privilege to know them too. The likes of Alf Wyman, a man of vision many years ahead of his time who had advocated leagues years before they were created. In fact he was largely responsible for persuading the Rugby Union to recognise the difference between what were then called "gate-taking clubs" and the rest.

Harry Walker was Mr Cov who had Coventry blue running through his veins. For much of his time as an official he spent most weekends running the Extras, discovering many talented individuals from the Coventry junior clubs and schools.

We can blame the Covid-19 crisis for current misfortunes but I strongly believe that the game below international and Premiership level was largely abandoned by the RFU some years before the pandemic hit.

What a kick in the teeth that is for a club like Coventry FC, having for years provided talent for the British Lions, the England team, Wales, Ireland and Warwickshire and other counties.

And the club has through its players, officials and fans provided a vision for the game that should not be forgotten.

John Lamb

Chapter Twenty-Six

Super Seventies Revisited

Michael Austin

(Coventry Evening Telegraph former Rugby Correspondent)

G reat rugby clubs are made not born and hard graft, laced with inspiration and expertise on and off the field has taken Coventry back to a position of pre-eminence almost 150 years since it all began. Memories may fade and decades disappear into the mists of time but flashbacks to the 1970s, two successive Cup triumphs in the RFU Club Competition at Twickenham and an innovative style of rugby still shine brightly.

The pantheon of Cov internationals in that era featured some who should have won more caps while others, who were on the fringe of a breakthrough, didn't quite make it. At the head of that list was prop Jim Broderick, with 386 Cov appearances in 20 seasons. He toured Canada in 1967 and the Far East, also with England, four years later and was respected throughout the land. He made a monumental 44 appearances in 1972-73, the season when Cov beat Bristol 27-15 in the club's first Twickenham victory. In four campaigns from 1972-76 he totalled a whopping 132 matches, encompassing a second Cup triumph 26-6 over London Scottish and was a larger than life character with a soft centre and a sharp sense of humour.

When standing at the front of a line-out for the Barbarians against East Midlands in March 1974, Brodders gave me a wink and a grin in the old Northampton press box. Another day, he made me feel like the victim of a mugging while at a cash machine in High Street, Coventry. He grabbed me from behind, and grabbed my inside thigh before I realised the identity of the friendly 'culprit'. He even made a 'Houdini-style escape' during a travel break at the Severn Bridge services en route to Wales. Brodders suddenly jumped over a low brick wall to what seemed like a long drop into the estuary. Wrong! He landed on wide grassy bank and when everyone rushed over he was hiding behind the wall with 'gotcha' written all over his face. His passing, aged 65, in April 2009 after a long illness, was lamented by all.

People as well as playing performances are key to team harmony. They included Bill Gittings with his '5ft 7' club, with membership restricted to those of Bill's own height, Geoff Evans, who was a ferocious exponent of a physically painful game called 'knuckles' and Thumper Dingley. He would only answer to that forename, though in my days as the rugby correspondent of the *Coventry Evening Telegraph*, people used to ask what's his real name? "Thumper" insisted the former Trinity Guild prop. The word was it might be 'Arthur' but one of the world's great mysteries still remains unsolved.

Welshman Malcolm Lewis, Coventry's first official coach, in 1972-73, was a major influence on Coventry's ongoing success. That season brought 40 wins, a draw and nine defeats with record 1,153 points for and only 505 against − a success rate of 81%, statistically the best season of the decade. Malcolm was the 'best man' at my wedding, a role that he didn't take lightly. Everything was spot on which typified him. From 1972-79, my time span covering Cov, the matches I most anticipated were those against Moseley, London Welsh, Northampton, Gloucester and Bristol, along with the cross-border challenges from Cardiff, Llanelli, Swansea and Neath.

A regular surreal experience as a journalist was the impressive armful of Saturday night 'Pinks', priced at 3p, that arrived hot foot or rather hot 'vanned' from Corporation Street, post-match at Coundon Road. Within 80 minutes of the final whistle, spectators staying for a pint or two could read my 800-word report of Cov's fortunes that afternoon. Its speed of production was a masterpiece of 'old technology'. For me, the sight of the incoming news vendor allowed a pause for thought and a wait for feedback on whether the readers had watched the same game as me. Happily, more often than not they had.

Sometimes, I 'escaped' to the gents adjacent in the foyer for five minutes or so to let the dust settle.

One afternoon, I found myself standing there in the male preserve next to the great Harry Walker. "All right, Mike?" Harry enquired. "Yes thanks," I responded. A pause followed. "Well," he said. "You know when you said in the paper that Brian Holt dug the ball out of a ruck for the winning try, it wasn't. It was our Richard!" There was no answer to that, except it was in a distant corner on a murky day in the last minute and I was dictating copy down the phone at the time.

The demise of the Pink 'un' and in other geographical areas the Green 'un' or in rare instances the Blue 'un' signified the passing of time and that of Saturday night sports papers, together with the people that produced them. Sadly, they include Bob Cole, the talented, jovial and much loved *Coventry Telegraph* photographer, who died last year and Lou Morris. They took almost all the newspaper's rugby images for many a year. Gone but not forgotten.

On the nights when no-one outside Warwickshire could access the *PINK*, Cov were usually playing in distant parts and returning home late, sometimes very, very late. My first away match covering the 'Blue and Whites' – don't call them that an irate reader wrote – was at Bridgend. I'd booked in at the Coventry YMCA as a temporary home, clambered off the coach at Coundon Road around 2.45am after the return journey, hiked across the precinct and found my lodgings in total darkness, locked and bolted. In desperation, I found an unsecured ground floor window, opened it and climbed in, expecting to find an arresting hand on the back of my shoulder. The Coventry Central Police station was only just around the corner at Little Park Street but all was well, especially as Cov had won 18-11 at the Brewery Field. By then, that had seemed about two days earlier.

Life on the Cov coach, driven by the highly popular 'Texas Bob', was never dull. When match secretary Alf Wyman, 'Mr Coventry', walked down the aisle, handing out a meal allowance of around £1.50 to each player, a song broke out "Get your money out Alfie" to the tune of

"What's it all about, Alfie." The other party ditty when it came to the venerable former hooker buying drinks, was "A double Wyman works wonder, works wonders", mimicking the advertising jingle of "A double diamond works wonders ..."

Sitting on the Cov coach, especially after a late night takeaway stop, can put you adjacent to some famous people. After one 'refuelling' venture in Wales, I found myself next to Colonel Sanders, the brand ambassador and symbol of Kentucky Fried Chicken, on the bus. I could have sworn he was outside the shop when we got off. Yes he was – a life-size cardboard cut-out, who was duly returned to his 'doorman duties' before the coach pulled away.

Then there was Béziers for a tournament also involving Cov, Glamorgan and Padua in September 1978. Multiple vineyards were on the itinerary but the nitty gritty was kicking off against Béziers, the French champions in six of the previous eight years. Cov lost 31-6 in a game that gave even deeper meaning to the word attritional. I got on the coach at Coundon Road for the drive to Gatwick and flight to Montpellier and thought: 'who is this diminutive player. I don't know'. The opening match hallmarked him as determined, unflinching and hard as nails. Bob Hobson, guesting from Barkers' Butts, took everything on his debut that his famous opposite number Alain Paco threw at him. Paco, the France Grand Slam hooker the previous year, won 35 Test caps and six French Championship titles which didn't impress Bob. He got on with the job against the odds, just like his teammates. Cov beat Padua 15-7 in their other game.

The most distant trip in my time involved a 516-mile journey to Hawick and back for a Friday evening match on April 6, 1973. At least that was the plan. Cov lost 18-13 at Mansfield Park but it was only part of the tale. Less than 24 hours later, England won an international tournament in Edinburgh that celebrated the Scotland RFU Centenary. It was the forerunner to the Rugby World Cup Sevens and England's nine-strong squad featured four Cov players – David Duckham, Peter Rossborough, Peter Preece and John Gray. Fran Cotton, later to join the club, led the side.

Ironically, the Cov team that played Hawick were due to stay two nights in the Scottish town and have a day trip to the historic event in which England beat Ireland 22-18 in the final. Other entrants were New Zealand, Australia, Scotland, France, Wales and the Scottish President's VII. But the proprietor of the Buccleuch Hotel, where the party was booked in, had imposed a draconian 10pm Friday night curfew, despite the final whistle for the Cov match being blown only two hours earlier.

When a few players and I turned up at 10.15pm after 'a knock up' the man in charge arrived at the front door wearing only a dressing down and a face like thunder. No-one had the temerity to ask: "I don't suppose there's any chance of a nightcap?" It would have sent him into an apoplectic fit. The following morning, to everyone's surprise he asked us to leave and cancelled our Saturday night stay. We clambered on the coach ready to head back to Coventry, braving the frustration of missing the Murrayfield tournament that became a memorable Cov triumph as well as that of England. But the saga didn't end there...

No sooner had we left Hawick than someone picked up a newspaper and said: "Sale are at home to Gosforth this afternoon. Let's do a detour!" Both of those clubs had special friendships with Cov so you've guessed it. After a true Sale welcome and memories of past matches stirred by ample liquid refreshment, the coach rolled back into Coundon Road around 2.30 on the Sunday morning. What a magical mystery tour, the memory of which remains just as vivid 48 years on.

So does the impression that Alf (Wyman) made on me. We had daily early morning phone calls in the quest to get Cov stories on the back page of the *Evening Telegraph*'s lunchtime edition. Positive news was always the target and Alf was always totally honest about things. When something negative turned up he didn't hide it but knew I would deal with it sensibly. One of my predecessors rang Alf one Friday morning near deadline time but he was out doing his day job as a painter and decorator. Alf's supremely supportive wife Ivy took the call. When asked who was replacing the injured player that had cried off at short notice Ivy said: "Oh dear. Alf's not here and I don't know who I'm going to put in."

The bottom line is that I covered 286 Cov matches in England, Wales, Scotland, Ireland and France. What wonderful seven seasons they were. By far, the best newspaper editor I've had in my career was Keith Whetstone at the *Evening Telegraph*, who showed vision, enterprise and integrity as well as being a devout rugby man. He said, hopefully with tongue in cheek, when we shared a return flight to Birmingham from a France-England match in Paris: "I'm signing your expenses for this – I must be mad!" He also sent me to cover the final three weeks of the British & Irish Lions epic, unbeaten tour of South Africa in 1974 for the newspaper during which I was able to share in the experiences of Geoff Evans and Fran Cotton, Cov's players on the trip. I also top scored with 41 for the British Press against the British Lions in an end-of-tour cricket match at the Wanderers Club in Johannesburg but that's another story. Happy days!

Mike Austin sharing memories with John 'Cruncher' Gray.

Majestic Cov

Chapter Twenty-Seven

True as Coventry Blue

Michael Austin

(Coventry Evening Telegraph former Rugby Correspondent)

Red and green are the traditional colours of the City of Coventry but the club's roots are deeply entrenched in blue, the hue the side adopted from the very beginning of its existence in 1874. Alongside that, early team groups show Coventry wearing much narrower hoops than those of modern times.

Styles have changed and originally there was a lack of TRUE AS COVENTRY BLUE when shirts were difficult to obtain. Some Coventry players wore buttoned-necked jerseys and others sported ones with round necks. The switch to broader hoops came at the turn of the 20th century but there were other variations as the professional era beckoned.

An experiment using jerseys without collars in the soccer mould in the late 1960s was a throwback to the club's earliest days. The Rotherham family, who played for the club around the turn of the 20th century, was renowned for an ability to produce a perfect 'Coventry Blue' at their Spon Street works.

The history of such a distinctive colour dates back to the 16th century when Coventry was renowned for a thread dyed by a special process that ensured it did not fade. For the previous 100 years, the Dyers' Company had been using woad, a plant whose leaves, when crushed and boiled, yield a deep fast blue dye. Coventry Blue developed from this with the process being carried out at Spon End, adjacent to the River Sherbourne and only a short walk from the Butts Park Arena.

The Old Dyers Arms, a public house, still stands close by and, appropriately, is well patronised by local rugby players. Coventry Blue was famous enough to be mentioned by 17th century writers notably Ben Jonson, one of whose characters said in 1621: "I have lost my skein of Coventry Blue." In another play five years later, the words: 'Though his hue be not of Coventry Blue' appeared. Michael Drayton, a poet born in Hartshill, Nuneaton in the Elizabethan era, also refers to 'His breech of Coventry Blewe' in 'Dowsabell'.

The proverbial saying 'True as Coventry Blue' became well known and the Coventry Leet Book, the mayor's register, listed many regulations designed to protect the trade from fraudulent practices. Counterfeit thread was still made inside and outside Coventry and before the end of Elizabeth I's reign the genuine article had been discredited and the industry fell into decline.

For many years, Tom Pollard, a sports outfitter, was in charge of obtaining jerseys to Coventry's specifications from a supplier in Nottingham. Jim Stewart and Rodney Webb, eminent former Coventry players, also provided shirts with change strips usually in plain blue or white until the 1990s.

The club's original badge was the city's own coat of arms that was supplemented after the Second World War. In 1959, the Eagle of Leofric, the husband of Lady Godiva, and the phoenix rising from the flames were introduced. These are the symbols of old and new Coventry. The city's motto 'Camera Principis' means the 'Prince's Chamber' and is believed to mark the link between Edward the Black Prince and the city. Cheylesmore Manor, a medieval house in Coventry, was once owned by his grandmother, Queen Isabella, and it eventually passed to him.

This wonderful old photograph dates to 1874 – the year the Coventry club was founded. It is a precious image … yet it was rescued from a skip!

For the record, the line-up of the team on the photograph salvaged by Spike O'Donnell is:

Back row: J. Wright, F. Haynes, A. Ratliff, S. Cash, H. Ratliff (capt), C. Waters, W. Warman, G. Ratliff.

Middle row: F. Ratliff, J.S. Clarke, C. Perkins, H. Walters, W.J. Kettle.

Front row: F. Browett, W.F. Wyley, J. Wanklyn.

Majestic Cov

Spike, who died in 2008, was a key figure in the Former Players' Association and helped establish their pavilion – an old school classroom – at the Moseley Avenue end of the ground. He made his debut for Cov in 1952 as a 16 stone six-footer in the second-row. He made 109 appearances for the club. His debut was against Gloucester. He once recalled : "Harry Walker played in that game and he gave a pre-match team talk. I was a relative youngster and I didn't know who to be more afraid of – the Gloucester pack, or H." Spike came close to an Irish cap. Working at Rootes Motors, he was selected for an Ireland trial in Dublin. He finished his night shift at Rootes in the early morning, cycled home, got washed and changed, and then caught a taxi to Elmdon Airport before flying to Dublin. By all accounts, he had a good trial – but was not selected for the Ireland XV. He returned home that evening and reported for the night shift an hour late. He was given a telling off by his boss!

Another stalwart former player was No 8 John Gardiner, who gave so much of his time to his beloved club, acting as groundsman and carrying out repairs around the ground. The loyalty of ex-players like Spike, John and many others was an expression of devotion to the Coventry club. Ben Gulliver who, like his father, Tony, donned the Cov jersey, recalls: "I have vivid memories of John Gardiner. He was groundsman at Coundon Road. I would have been aged between five and 10. After watching the old man play, I'd spend hours out on the field playing. John would always leave one floodlight on for me, even when all my mates had gone home. I'd eventually be dragged off the field covered head to toe in mud. Such great memories of a great man."

Brian 'Spike' O'Donnell

John Gardiner
Photo: Tony Dickenson

Chapter Twenty-Eight

Eighties Exposed: Bare bottoms, black-balling and Bermuda

Steve Evans

(Coventry Evening Telegraph Rugby Correspondent 1979-1987)

There is an unwritten rule among rugby players. It is akin to one of the game's Ten Commandments. "What goes on on tour stays on tour" is a doctrine religiously adhered to. Well, sometimes.

Risking the perils of punishment, I am going to break that code of silence and take myself back to Coventry's tour of Bermuda in 1980.

Look away now, ladies, for at least the next few paragraphs.

She was a Bermudian heiress with her own yacht and a kinky liking for bodily-adorned Peanut Butter. Let's just say I inherited some of the heiress's hairs which I promptly plonked inside an England's Glory matchbox as a keepsake and to prove to the lads that I had been a naughty nocturnal boy overlooking Hamilton Harbour.

Suddenly, it was 4am and I was late for my pre-arranged call from the *Coventry Evening Telegraph* offices to dictate my match report. I clambered astride my hired 50cc Puch moped and rode back to my digs. The phone was ringing.

"Where have you been?" asked the copy-taker sitting at her typewriter with her headphones on. It was lovely Marjorie, my colleague and the mother of Coventry captain Paul Knee. "Err, I had a puncture," I lied.

Some years later, my new bride and I were invited to Trinity Guild's annual dinner. Fellow Bermuda tourist Thumper Dingley (ex-Guild) was there. He turned up at our table with a prezzie.

He'd been to the loo and plucked some hair from his South Pole region and placed the curly-wurlys in a presentation matchbox for me. The wife looked bemused.

I wriggled out of an awkward moment by smiling and saying: "What goes on on tour stays on tour."

That Bermuda tour at the end of my first season threw up some other memorable images.

I will always remember a tipsy Roy Freemantle falling asleep on the lawn at Bermuda Police Club, hugging "FD", the toy rabbit mascot. Why was he called FD? Because the youth team had won it weeks earlier after playing several games of prize bingo and the rabbit had cost them "f***ing dear."

The police club lawn was also the scene of a Kangaroo Court involving fly-half Chris Ison, who had scored 5 tries in one match. It was a trumped-up charge, of course, but out came the Cherry Blossom boot polish and Ison's trousers were removed for a sentence of black-balling.

The renowned pop singer and chef, Don Fardon, a proud Coventry kid who was part of the touring party, spent half-an-hour in the police cells. We'd set him up, telling him to ring the ship's bell hanging at the front of the police club bar. He rang it. What he didn't know was that it meant drinks all round or a spell in the cells.

It should have been long-serving centre Paul Coulthard's farewell tour. He ended up in hospital after his moped hit a wall, grazing his face.

Twenty-six of us were on mopeds, including alikados like Harry Walker, George Cole and club doctor Peter Brown. After Paul Coulthard's mishap, Mal Malik rang my digs and asked me not to mention the accident nor the mopeds, because it would worry those back at home. I obliged. What goes on on tour stays on tour, right?

Doc Brown had an unforgettable flight on the outward Jumbo Jet journey to Mexico, via Bermuda. No sleeping on tour was a mantra, but the good doctor was, well, soon in the land of zzzzzzzzz.

The lads asked one of the air hostesses for her make-up bag and gently put lipstick and other cosmetic adornments on his face. When he woke up, unaware of his appearance, he was told that Olympic runner Filbert Bayi was sitting alone not too far in front of him.

Doc Brown promptly plonked himself alongside Bayi and engaged in serious conversation, blissfully oblivious to the howls of laughter from the cabin crew, the players, oh, and the perplexed look on the face of the world-renowned athlete.

Tours are one thing. Away days are another.

I learned one thing back in the 80s. Never sit on the back seat of a Harry Shaw coach.

We were returning from a match in London. A few miles up the M1, Steve Brain walked down the aisle and pleaded with the driver to stop the coach. In his Brummie accent, he left the driver in no doubt about the urgency. "I need a shit … NOW", he boomed.

The driver pulled over onto the hard shoulder with his hazard lights on and Brainy mounted the grass embankment and did his business. He used his underpants to wipe his backside. When he "mooned" at the lads back on the coach, they noticed a large skid mark across his right butt cheek, so a Kleenex tissue was produced to wipe it off.

The tissue was then passed mouth-to-mouth all the way up the coach until it reached me on the back seat. "Right, Scribble. You're the last man. Swallow it!" As I said, the back seat harbours hidden perils.

In my first season, I bared my bum after a match at Cardiff Arms Park to join the fabled ranks of HITAG – the Hole In The Arse Gang and my first visit to Lansdowne Road for a game against Dublin Wanderers also involved someone dropping their trousers.

159

Huw Davies, destined to win 20 England caps, had just joined Cov. The newcomer was in for an initiation on the lawn of one of the Wanderers officials in front of our Irish hosts and their wives.

It was a Kangaroo Court. Again with a trumped-up charge. I was on the jury and we retired to the potting shed to consider our verdict in just one second. "Guilty", we declared.

Jim Broderick was the judge. He put a black flower-pot on his head to announce sentencing. Huw was stripped of his trousers and forced to sit on a chair while every member of the jury gave him a willy-whipping. Ouch – and welcome to Cov!

I recite these tales to illustrate that while Cov played hard on the field, they also played hard off it. They built a brotherhood and a camaraderie that I had never experienced in my sportswriting pilgrimage which started at Nuneaton RFC and ended at Coventry City FC.

It was while at Cov that, in 1983, I was named Britain's Provincial Sports Writer of the Year. I claim no boastful credit because it was truly Cov-inspired. The lads I met and wrote about during the years 1979-1987 were a true inspiration. In short, those were the best eight seasons of my 42-year journalistic journey.

I reluctantly left Coundon Road after being "promoted" to cover the FA Cup-winning Sky Blues. I have always retained my belief that there is a two-inch difference between the rugby player and the soccer player of my era – and it had nowt to do with the size of the male appendage.

Put your thumb on your breast-bone and your index finger over to the left. Two inches. That's all. Those Cov lads played from the heart. Those who embraced the other code played from the wallet.

It has been a pleasure, an honour to write this book about Cov.

To this fabulous club, I say thanks for the memories. And to Erica Roe, who semi-streaked to show the best two points ever seen at Twickenham, I say thanks for the mammaries.

* This book would not have happened without the unstinting and unwavering support of former player Simon Maisey, a centurion in terms of tries scored, and Alan Joseph, a half-centurion in terms of years supporting Cov. I salute them both and extend my heartfelt gratitude to two wonderful men who have Coventry FC (RU) etched on their souls. And maintaining the bare-bottomed theme, I'm sure they have the club tattooed on their butt cheeks ... C on the left and V on the right. So when they bend over, it spells CoV !!!

*Even on Test Match duty at Edgbaston, a scribbler needs his gallon of "inspiration"
(naughtily placed in front of me by a devilish snapper). Please note my summer
attire, which includes my faithful winter flat cap which protected me from Coundon
Road's rusty dandruff.*

Chapter Twenty-Nine

Cherished Times at Cov

Darrell Giles

(Coventry Evening Telegraph 1987 - 1993)

I arrived in Coventry in early 1987 fresh from covering a lengthy New Zealand tour of South Africa. Professional rugby was off and running in the southern hemisphere and the All Black and Springboks had embraced this new approach.

But I stepped into a winter of discontent as England and the other rugby-playing nations of the northern hemisphere struggled with the concept and it remained in the "too hard" basket for the time being.

The players down under were the new elite. If anything, it created or enlarged the gap between rugby writer and those players.

That was one thing I immediately noted on my arrival at Cov. The scribe was like a member of the extended First XV. To me, that was different and difficult. Not to mention I was following in the footsteps of the ultimate rugger bugger writer, Steve Scribble Evans, a legend behind the typewriter and telephone in those parts.

Professionalism, in a rugby sense, was not a word Scribble or the Cov lads had encountered much I dare say. But I do say that with the utmost respect as Steve-O was a professional with the pen. He came up with the nickname Wiki ... Kiwi backwards [pronounced Weekee) instead of Keewee].

Cov were Kings, or perhaps at the end of that era when I arrived, and in my humble opinion, their success over the years played a part in the early downfall from the new rugby Premier league.

The winter program consisted of matches against the best in Wales and the other top clubs in England. The matches over the border were always a treat and I think Cov regarded them as significantly bigger and better than any against their homeland opposition.

Cov dismissed a defeat to an English side in a different fashion to one against a Welsh XV. In a not too dissimilar vein, playing for Warwickshire seemed to lift the players more than turning out for Cov.

Mind you, that happens here in Queensland where I now reside as Brisbane Broncos rugby league players always lift a notch or two when playing State of Origin matches for Queensland against New South Wales. The annual criticism has come home to roost with the once-were-kings Broncos claiming a first NRL wooden spoon in 2020 while the Queensland side won the origin crown again.

I digress. I do remember then Cov coach Peter Rossborough, lovely chap, once taking me aside and in his most pleasant manner telling me that I was too critical of the players in my match reports … that they were not professionals. Fair criticism.

But there in lay the problem, few players and clubs in the UK wanted to make that next step. Some did: the Bath, Harlequins, Wasps and Leicesters of the rugby world. But Cov did not and they were left remembering the old glory days.

It was a common conversation at Coundon Road: did I know so-and-so who played for England in 19 something. I imagine it made it tough for the new breed of Cov players living up to those mighty reputations.

Ah Coundon Road, fond memories. Where you could get a rust shower for free with every Steve Thomas kick to touch crashing on the crumbling roof. A metaphor for the times.

I have many great memories from my six seasons covering Cov. I enjoyed conversations in the tour bus, with the brains in the backs, Martin Fairn & Co, to some more earthy chats with the pack. They were, as we say down under, salt-of-the-earth blokes who loved those 80 minutes rucking and mauling, and those 80 or more minutes afterwards sinking a pint.

And there were some darn fine players: the Thomas lads, Jason Minshull, Rob Hardwick, Julian Hyde, Neil Back (briefly) … just to name a few.

I loved my time in Coventry. I can honestly say after 40-plus years in the journalism game, covering everything from crime, to politics, to now in council land, that time was cherished. I loved the immediacy of Saturday afternoons filing over the phone to *The PINK* and seeing my words in print minutes later.

There were many great times travelling with the Cov lads: to an England match against then Five Nations opponents France in Paris where those said miscreants introduced me to some of the interesting experiences one can indulge in along the Moulin Rouge.

And then there was Dublin. The infamous tour to the Irish capital to take on the Wanderers. We nearly didn't get into the place as some Cov wag told a customs officer that a colleague had a bomb in his bag. I gathered it was not a word you mentioned in those parts.

I can't remember much of the match itself. I do recall all the off-field highlights. I had to give a speech in front of a Wanderers clubhouse full of drunken rugger buggers. About halfway through I copped a bread roll soaked in Guinness that had been thrown with more accuracy that a Thomo pass to his No 10 that day. The beer bread hit the side of my head but I rolled on with my speech, hardly missing a word.

There was the willy whipping episode. All of Dublin's elite at a BBQ thrown by the Irish RFU president … and I had to get my wonker out. Impressive as it may have been, it was not something I usually did, shy lad that I was, and probably the last thing many of those lovely ladies expected or wanted to see. I don't know what sin I had committed but the Cov jury found me guilty (something harsh I wrote no doubt) and the old fella was held by one of the lads (I can't remember who had that rough touch) and I got six whips from a tree branch (likely a leaf or something small).

But I had the last laugh! At another Dublin function Godber and Gully literally hauled me up on stage and my punishment this time was to drink a pint of mixed spirits. I was not a big drinker by any stretch and that pint of poison would have killed me. But the GGs took their eye off the prize momentarily and I grabbed a pint of beer that was sitting beside the spirits and sculled it in record time with huge applause from the crowd, who thought I had down the spirits. Legend status from that point on.

Darrell Giles

Chapter Thirty

The Campaigning Journalist Who Saved Cov from the Abyss

John Wilkinson

(Coventry Telegraph staff writer 1989-2008; freelance correspondent 2008-2018; former club media officer)

My first Coventry game was the 1975-76 John Player Cup tie away at Kettering and with my notebook firmly in the home camp as a rookie reporter on the local *Evening Telegraph*.

I don't recall too much about the game, which Cov won 20-12, other than being somewhat in awe of all the England internationals and triallists either playing or watching.

A few years later I was sent to Coundon Road to cover a game between Cov and Northampton, I recall Cov winning the game, but my abiding memory is of the raucous support and banter emitting from the Cowshed, coupled with being showered in rust when the ball landed on the roof of the main stand and the generous help I was given by erstwhile colleague, and friend, John Butler.

I joined the *Coventry* (then *Evening*) *Telegraph* in September 1989 as number two rugby man. Darrell Giles was the Cov writer then, so my early involvement was as his deputy – starting with an Easter game away to Headingley, notable only for Steve Thomas talking his way into a red card as the referee tired of his incessant chatter, and including a trip to Dublin for the Wanderers weekend. As the newbie I feared for my safety, having heard tales of previous tours, but I must have held my end up pretty well as in his speech on the Sunday afternoon tour of the Tullamore Dew distillery, I remember Harry Walker, in his wrapping up speech, growling "... and we've had a new Press man with us, Wilkinson – he must be okay because you b*****s haven't done anything to him." I'd arrived!

After Darrell moved on, the Cov position passed to me and I quickly became aware of the weight of expectation linked to such an illustrious past.

The following years were a real roller coaster ride of emotions through the eras of Gerry Sugrue, Keith Fairbrother and Andrew Green, leading up to the remarkable events of the summer of 2008.

I was well aware of the depth of feeling for the club, both in the city and the rugby world as a whole, but it really came through in those few short weeks in June and July.

It was a tough time, and having entered administration in February that year and re-emerged as a new company, Cov – who had finished the season in mid-table in National League One (now the Championship) – were asked to fulfil a number of requirements before being allowed to start the 2008-09 season, not least posting a bond of £100,000 as surety against further financial problems.

Despite repeated assurances from owner Andrew Green that investment was on the way, as the deadline approached it became increasingly clear that the money wasn't coming.

The RFU management board was meeting at 3.30pm on June 13th (a Friday!) when the decision would be made – no bond, and Cov's playing share would be withdrawn.

If that happened, to continue playing Cov would go to the very bottom of the league pyramid and it would effectively have been the end of the great club.

It was around 1.30pm when I took a call at my desk from a contact at the RFU. The money wasn't there and the meeting would rubber-stamp Cov's expulsion.

I had to write the story, but it was far too depressing to do it in the office, surrounded by others, so I decided to go home. The 20-minute drive set me thinking – 134 years of history going down the pan, the glory years of cup triumphs, all the Coventry internationals ... surely it couldn't be allowed to happen without a fight?

So I quickly composed an e-mail to Martyn Thomas, the chairman of the RFU management board, asking if the bond could be raised independently from the club, would the RFU reconsider?

Just after 3.30pm my phone rang. It was Martyn Thomas. How did I propose to raise the money? My reply was through a *Telegraph*-led public appeal and with the goodwill of the Coventry people and the respect that the name of Cov still commanded.

Amazingly, he said he would give me until that evening to put some concrete plans in writing and would reconvene the board meeting, via conference call, on Saturday. I was to ring him at 1pm.

I then drove back to the *Telegraph*, knocked on editor Alan Kirby's door, and – with a deal of trepidation - told him that I wanted to commit the newspaper to raising the money. Happily, without hesitation, he jumped on board.

Some ideas were put together, I e-mailed Martyn Thomas, and rang him as agreed the next day. The decision, he said, was not unanimous, but as chairman he had the final say and we had the green light with two weeks in which to raise the bond.

On Monday the *Telegraph* launched the campaign, and that was when the Coventry people stood up to be counted. What happened was extraordinary.

By then I had involved club stalwart John Butler and playing legend Peter Rossborough, and after a couple of days a building society account had been opened and trustees appointed.

The two weeks, which the RFU let run into three because of the time it took to get up and running, were a blur. So many people stepped forward to help, events were organised, and boosted by television and newspaper coverage the donations poured in from Coventry, Warwickshire and all corners of the rugby community.

It included an unforgettable Saturday in the city's Lower Precinct where we had been given space for a stall and bucket collection. A number of players came along to join an army of supporters, and after nine hectic hours and a few more counting, bagging and weighing, the amount raised was well over £2,000.

I particularly recall one man saying that watching his son play in a Coventry Schools cup final at Coundon Road was one of the proudest moments of his life and because of this the future of the club meant so much to him. And the little lad who insisted that his mum put his pocket money for that week in the bucket.

By July 2 the fund stood at just over £52,000 (it eventually reached £54,783). Short of the target, but in the time and circumstances a terrific achievement and accepted as such by the RFU.

The news that Cov could continue playing was confirmed, somewhat fittingly, at a meeting of National One club representatives at Butts Park Arena that afternoon.

Of course, it wasn't the end of Coventry's financial woes and two seasons later the club again entered administration and was relegated. But by then the right people were in place to step in and put the club on a firm footing to move forward which, with Jon Sharp's subsequent appointment as chairman, has taken it to where it stands today.

What those few weeks did prove was just how much support and pride there is for the club and how much it means to so many people.

Here are just a few of the many memorable moments during my time.

The unforgettable 19-18 win over Newcastle in November 1996 with Coundon Road packed to the rafters, in a season which saw Cov get to within 40 minutes of the now Premiership but was also the prelude to uncertain times.

The 102-22 home win over Nottingham when the Coundon Road scoreboard operator had to find and hammer in an extra nail, much to the amusement of the crowd.

Taking a call late one afternoon from Keith Fairbrother, suggesting I may like to go to training that night as he had just signed Zinzan Brooke. Sure enough, there was the legendary All Black No. 8, and what a class act he proved to be, on and off the pitch, over the two seasons he was here.

Waiting for a game at Wakefield to start when Fairbrother and Ian Carvell came up to the Press box to tell me that the club had just taken over Bedford. A couple of days later a bewildered bus load of Bedford players assembled at Coundon Road where the future was outlined to them – it was to be a way into the Premiership for Cov. It didn't happen, the outraged people of Bedford rallied round to keep the club at Goldington Road, but full marks for Cov's audacity.

Again at Wakefield, the winner-take-all relegation decider when Shaun Perry's early try proved decisive in the result that kept Cov up and, a few months later, saw Wakefield disappear. Such fine margins in those times.

The final game of the 2002-03 season when a last-minute Luke Smith penalty gave a young and injury-ravaged Cov a totally unexpected 26-25 win over Rotherham, confirmed as champions and waiting to be presented with the league trophy. Talk about party poopers.

And more recently, the stunning 42-0 win at Darlington Mowden Park in February 2018 which all but wrapped up the National Division One title and promotion back to the Championship after ten long years – a position confirmed a month later at Caldy in a flurry of snow and with five games still to go.

John Wilkinson

Chapter Thirty-One

Fifty Years of Memories of Watching Cov

Alan Joseph

(Loyal Supporter for over 50 Years)

The day David Duckham sent JPR Williams scurrying off towards the pub will live long in my memory. At least, in my mind's eye, that's what appeared to happen.

The Wales full-back, facing Duckham in a game against Cov at Coundon Road, had bought a trademark, outrageous dummy and sidestep and I swear he ended up over the touchline and over the road and into the Coundon pub car park.

Maybe, just maybe, JPR felt like downing a swift one to drown his sorrows because Mr Duckham had just scored a memorable try.

David was one of those once in a lifetime players who was unstoppable, whether playing for Cov, England, Baa Baas or British Lions. He once scored six tries in one game for The Lions in 1971. His Man of the Match performance in the Baa Baas vs All Blacks classic in 1973 will never ever be forgotten. David was by far the greatest of all the players I have seen at Cov. A truly spectacular performer.

Peter Preece (at eleven stone surely the best pound for pound player ever to wear the blue and white or Red Rose jersey), British Lion Geoff Evans and Chris Wardlow weaving their midfield magic after quality ball from the forwards passed on by Dick Cowman and Bill Gittings at half back, creating space so wingers Rodney Webb, Simon Maisey, Nobby Bolton, Paul Knee and Duckham himself would all amass over 100 tries each. Behind them one of the finest of running full backs Peter Rossborough running from deep in open play with his deceptive pace, jink and step was a stunningly glorious sight to see. Another player to reach the 100 try mark.

And it is with Peter that my story begins ...

We both started Woodlands school on the same day in 1971. Peter was my English teacher and I was eleven years old. Free tickets were given out to the school so we headed off to see `Sir` play for Cov at Coundon Road.

I have been involved with Cov ever since.

As I said previously, that all international back line was spectacular but the forwards, as always, provided good ball.

The magnificent all round sportsman John `Cruncher` Gray, Jim Broderick, Ian Darnell, John Barton, Roger Creed, Brian Holt, Richard Walker, Fran Cotton, John Gallagher, Keith Fairbrother, Barry Ninnes , Ron Jones were dominant.

The two Cup Final wins and The Centenary game against The Baa Baas in 1974 were special memorable occasions too. That Cov team was possibly the best club side in the world at that time. Five Cov players were in the first England team to win against The All Blacks in New Zealand, and five players in the England 7's squad to become World Champions in 1973.

In the 80s Cov had yet another truly formidable pack. The physicality of those forwards was immense. The names run off the tongue, Lee Johnson, Steve Brain, Steve Wilkes, Tony Gulliver, Brian Kidner and the huge back row trio of Graham Robbins, Paul Thomas and Dick Travers were a match for any in Cov's history. A formidable group of men.

Not forgetting the much missed Andy Farrington who was an integral part of that group of players.

Godber and Leebone still hold the try scoring records for their positions. In the backs, Stuart `Louie` Hall and `Electric` Eddie Saunders ran in tries from everywhere.

I was fortunate enough to go on Cov's tour with that brilliant back row of Robbins, Thomas and Travers to Bermuda in 1985. Godber, Mad Dog and Dick were a magnificent trio of tough, hard as nails players and wonderful men.

Drinking Dark and Stormy's for three weeks with Godber was obviously the perfect way to train as, within months, he took his rightful place in The England team. The three-week tour is still talked about till this day. Superb performances on the pitch including 5 tries in half an hour for Louie against The Mariners Club, but most importantly making friends for life. Memorable trip!

At scrum half, Steve Thomas was the player who in my humble opinion the most complete player I have seen in my 50 years at Cov. He could pass, kick, tackle, run as well as anyone. A tough competitor. Quite why he didn't collect any caps has always been a surprise to many. It was always great to watch him cajole his forwards whilst chatting to the referee.

The 80's team were amongst the top three or four in the country and were unlucky to miss out on a Cup Final several times. The team even found time to appear on TISWAS with Chris Tarrant hours before an important game and still won easily!

Another great occasion was The Sport Aid 7s in 1986. Cov Youth Team lost very narrowly to the 1st team in the final in front of a huge crowd. A memorable day.

During the 70s and 80s there were several trips each season to South Wales to watch Cov play against all the top Welsh sides. I well remember the 76-9 defeat at Cardiff, the late night draw there after the Cov coach broke down on the way to the game, Peter Rossborough beating the points in a season record at Ebbw Vale , Lee Johnson scoring a spectacular `Basher` move try at Pontypool, arriving at Maesteg and Neath to find games called off due to frozen pitches in the days before mobile phones. There were many journeys at that time to see very physical and sometimes brutal games refereed by a local official. After several years without a win in Wales Cov won at Pontypridd. Only three

Cov supporters were there and we partied long into the night in their clubhouse and then our car ran out of petrol on the way home!

Later came the sides with more tough forwards like Julian Hyde, Gareth Tregilgas, Trevor Revan, Lee Crofts, Dave Addleton, and the magnificent Danny Grewcock who just oozed class and menace. Tony Gulliver and Danny Grewcock must both have been a nightmare to play against. Two wonderful 2^(nd) rows. Julian Horrobin and Derek Eves worked magnificently well together. Julian was a complete footballer. His tackle on Tim Stimpson at West Hartlepool is imprinted on the mind of anyone who was there that day and his tap and go move with Eves always brought the Cowshed noise level up several notches. Mick Curtis and Jason Minshull were powerful in the centres.

The wins against an All Star Newcastle side and the home leg win in the Play Off against London Irish were both games that will always be remembered by those who were there.

A couple of years ago was a record breaking promotion winning season – 1200 points and 183 tries. A crowd of 4,000 at the last game.

I was fortunate and proud to be involved behind the scenes on the Committee for many years and Social Club Secretary too. It was an honour to serve with British Lions Ivor Preece, Peter Jackson, David Duckham and many others who only wanted the best for our Club. I played a few games in the Youth Team (when I was in my mid 20s!) due to a shortage of players and guested for Northampton against Cov Extras at Coundon Road. Northampton won. I was a useless, hopeless player.

The future is bright with Jon Sharp leading us onwards and upwards with his generosity and drive. A very bright future with many plans in place but I believe it is always good to look back from time to time at our rich history of so many magnificent players and games and of everyone involved in any way over the last 147 years of OUR GREAT CLUB.

Alan Joseph

Chapter Thirty-Two

My Life and Times at Coventry Rugby

John Butler
(Club Historian who has compiled the players' records)

I just wonder how many people reading this will associate with me and say to themselves "If there was one particular moment in life or element when, if I could, I would change it?"

It is a question often asked, in my particular case, is something I have always felt very strongly about.

My biggest regret is not being in a position to don the famed blue and white jersey of Cov. Circumstances decreed that was never going to happen, but had things been different, I would have valued and treasured it well above an England shirt and several others. The nearest point I ever reached was running the line for Alf Wyman when he was Match Secretary, but actually that did see me run out at Twickenham when Cov visited Harlequins.

The circumstances I refer to relate to the back injury I was born with, which has always limited me in a physical and sporting sense. I am however so grateful to the doctors in Coventry all those 78 years ago for all they did for me from the very outset.

It helps me to explain however how from a very young age my passion for all things Cov Rugby developed.

Whilst one grandfather was very much a Coventry City supporter, the rest of the immediate family were very much Rugby minded. My Dad took me to Coundon Road at the end of the 1947/48 season to see Cov play Old Blues and from there I was hooked.

When I look back now to those early days, I am truly reminded of the names of just some of the many greats that Cov Rugby produced. Harold Greasley, Club captain, who through my uncle who worked with him, helped to fill my first autograph book. Harold was later to become President of the Supporters Club.

Ivor Preece, Norman Stock, Harry Walker, John Gardiner, Ray Batstone. The list is endless. Unfortunately, I am just not quite old enough to remember the famed three Wheatley Bros playing!

Those early days of mine though in the 50s, just like decades to follow, saw Cov Rugby have many real ups and just a few downs. Full Back Ted Hewitt was my first boyhood hero, capped just twice for England, but captain actually when Cov lost 15 games on trot in 1953. I thought at the time the world was coming to an end! Then just after came Peter Jackson, a real legend if ever there was one.

Peter when he arrived in 1954 from Old Edwardians had played for the Midlands v South Africa and he became the first real 'outsider' to join the Club. He of course went on to be capped for England and the British Lions, whilst also captaining the Club and serving both as Fixture and General Secretary.

Little did I know at the time, but on my first visit to Twickenham in 1958, that PBJ would score the winning try for the 14 man England in injury time v Australia – I lost my voice for a week. No replacements then! I am proud to say we became close personal friends as my involvement with the Club grew over the years.

Then when sadly in 2004 Peter passed away, I was asked by Jean his wife to give the eulogy at Peter's funeral. One of the proudest, but saddest days I can ever recall seeing, as I looked up, a sea of faces with so many greats of the game there in tribute. It truly was an honour.

It was Charlie Prescott actually who was my real mentor of those early days. As Secretary of the Supporters Club, it was he who received my letter to Club in 1955, saying simply "please can I sell programmes?"

Over the next 15 years or so, I moved from programme seller to joining the Supporters' Club Committee and becoming Secretary, then Chairman through the 1960's.

Fast forward to 1977 and by now married to Anne with two small boys, a career move to Staffordshire caused me to wonder if my Cov links might just end.

I had though been involved with local radio from 1972, when BBC Radio Birmingham approached the Club, looking for anyone who might be interested in commentating. Just myself and Mike McLean, he of the famed front row, put our hands up. For my part all these years later, I still passionately enjoy doing it.

Those early radio years coincided with Cov reaching the RFU Club Knock Out final twice, winning both v Bristol in 1973 and London Scottish 1974. For the second of those, there was no local radio coverage, with Radio Birmingham having no other station to share costs with!

It was Peter Sharp, Club Secretary in 1977 I recall, who enquired, "you have now settled into family life and your new job, how about joining the general Committee of the Club?" How could I refuse and it was straight into a role of Press and Publicity Officer.

Then, some eight years later, I arrived for a meeting to be told by Peter Jackson, now Secretary, "John Barton is standing down as Fixture Secretary, how do you fancy it?" A phone call home to Anne and there I was involved in what proved to be fascinating and challenging role. No text or emails then.

By now, I was also editing the Club match programme, the Fixture Secretary role though took on some 14 seasons. In 1984, just before leagues and the game going professional, Cov had traditionally run two sides, during my early years in the role, on board for a time came the Wanderers and Colts sides. Challenging it certainly was, but so rewarding.

Being a Fixture Secretary at the time was akin to being in "a club in itself". The camaraderie amongst colleagues was just immense. Looking back, I would not have missed it for the world.

The years that followed as League Rugby came about in 1987 were the least successful the Club had experienced for a long time. Peter Rossborough and myself have often felt that the death in 1982 of Alf Wyman, Match Secretary supreme, was a real turning point. Cov seemed to lose momentum. By the time leagues came into being, one season was all Cov achieved in League One (nowadays the Premiership) and little changed before the game turned professional in 1995.

At this point, my life and times with Cov took a very definite move from a family point of view. Sons Dave and Mike, each a scrum half, having come through the Colts, both made senior debuts. Dave, via Rugby Lions, where he found himself off the bench opposite Eddie Saunders and Mike at Moseley. To complete the 'young Butlers' involvement, about this time, daughter Ruth became the Club's first ever ball girl. Proud times. Not least as well when Mike a year or two later gained his 'blue' at Oxford.

Gerry Sugrue by now was Club Chairman and when I found myself made redundant in 1996, within weeks came a call for a meeting with Gerry. For some two-and-a-half years I suddenly found myself effectively being paid for what had been my hobby. Office Administration Manager for Cov, I could hardly believe it.

That particular game with Newcastle Falcons, which so many remember even now, with 8,000 packed into Coundon Road, plus the two match play off with London Irish came 1996/97, with Cov literally within minutes of returning to the Premiership.

The failure to achieve that though was at an expensive cost. By May 1998 Cov came close to folding which meant that the bailiffs would be brought in and, for myself, any active role within Cov Rugby for a while came to an end.

This period in time for me personally was also tough, with a heart attack being suffered in early 1999.

Fortunately, the rescue package applied saw the Club back in playing action for season 1998/99 and eventually the move away from Coundon Road to the Butts Park Arena in September 2004. Cov Rugby had come full circle, returning to its original home of the late 19th century, albeit with the pitch at a rather different angle.

By now I found myself editing the Club programme once again, whilst also serving a period on the Club's Advisory Board.

Another change of ownership, but unfortunately financial stability did not follow for long.

Early in the Summer of 2008, came a phone call from my old friend and colleague John Wilkinson. John, still Rugby Correspondent at the *Coventry Evening Telegraph* at the time, had earlier established that unless a rescue package was put together, the Club would fold. That summer is not one that could be forgotten easily, but with the support and backing of the *Telegraph* Editor, within the timescale laid down by the RFU, it was possible to put together a financial package that was considered acceptable. Little of that would have been possible however without the fantastic Coventry membership and support, plus other outside support.

For a while previously, I had been acting as deputy for the Club Chairman at Second Division Board Meetings, largely in London. It just so happened though that in late 2008, one such meeting had seen the venue change to the Butts Park. During the early afternoon came the news via a phone call that the RFU had accepted the financial package and we could breathe again!

Another change of ownership, with the Club as a result struggling again, but with the Advisory Board taking the initiative late in season 2009/10, liquidation was avoided.

Sadly though, relegation to National League One was to follow.

The eight seasons which followed in National One were a real eye opener. Some lovely, real old fashioned rugby venues being visited, with first Scott Morgan, the former Welsh International coming on board in 2012 as Head Coach. Stability at last with new Executive Chairman Jon Sharp at the helm. Coventry born and bred, with a real desire and commitment to drive the Club forward.

Then in September 2016 came the appointment of Rowland Winter in the new Director of Rugby role. By the end of 2017/18, the goal in reaching the Championship had been achieved, one year earlier than originally thought possible. It was back though to the glory days, a season which saw countless club league records smashed.

Two seasons back in the Championship and with Cov at the end of 2018/19 finishing higher than any other promoted club had achieved previously at that time.

Who though could have predicted the developments of season 2019/20. The season sadly cut short by COVID-19 pandemic. A scenario which affected so many phases in life.

From a Cov Rugby perspective, when I look back over the last 70 plus years of my life and times with the Club, now in my role of Club Historian, yes, given the chance and with hindsight, perhaps some things could have changed.

The one element for me personally though which will never change is that desire and wish to have worn the blue and white 1st XV jersey.

John Butler

Chapter Thirty-Three

Cov Were the Best Team in the Land

Brendan Gallagher
(The Rugby Post)

Accepting an invitation to pen a few words for this celebration of Coventry rugby was the easy bit but deciding what to write about has been the challenge.

My first instinct was to recall that famous day when Cov beat a star studded Newcastle at the dawn of professionalism back at Coundon Road of blessed memory. Rarely have I known a crowd more energised and into a game and you got a strong sense of what it had been like back in the Cov glory days.

My lasting memory from that day – I think I was the only scribe from a national newspaper present – is of a towering performance from a young Danny Grewcock – I'm afraid he was always going to be snapped up by a Premiership club after that. I also recall a fuming John Bentley getting sent off and a Newcastle forward, who had better remain anonymous – punching and battering the away dressing room door down when I had nipped down straight after the whistle for a few quotes.

But tempted as I am to revel in that wonderful afternoon I am going to ponder on an early image that stuck with me as a young schoolboy in the 70s when I used to devour my monthly edition of Rugby World when it arrived. And that is the famous shot of eleven Coventry England internationals posing at Coundon road in their national kit ahead of the 1973-74 season.

I understand it was Alf Wyman – who made over 400 first team appearances but was working as the groundsman – at the time who

189

organised the picture. It would certainly need somebody of his stature to persuade 11 blokes to turn up in their nicely ironed England shirt at the right time on the right day.

It was a remarkable picture which spoke of a mighty club in its pomp and we need to bear in mind that two further England internationals were unavailable, away on their hols and the legendary – in my eyes anyway – John Gray just missed out having signed professional just a couple of weeks earlier.

When you start digging into it the picture is a fascinating snapshot and inspires all kinds of thoughts.

Firstly although we have become used in modern times to professional teams, with the ability to 'buy-in' anybody they want, fielding sides packed with internationals it was extremely unusual – freakish even – for an amateur club to boast such a vast array of talent at the time.

First and foremost it was down to home grown talent or well-established links with local schools, junior clubs, and Loughborough University up the road while it should also be noted that a good relationship with the local education authorities was always advisable. Rugby playing teachers was the richest seam of all to be mined by ambitious clubs in the 70s and 80s.

Another quirky observation, and perhaps the angle of the picture has something to do with it, but all eleven seem much of a muchness in terms of size and shape. This is like looking at a Rugby League line-up. No real extremes of width and height.

I was speaking to Keith Fairbrother recently and something he said struck a chord. He was explaining that with the strong Loughborough Uni influence at the time and with the glittering array of backs they reckoned to be the fittest, fastest, team in the country by some distance. And to maximise that the club drilled the young ball boys on the touchlines to ensure a ball was always available almost instantly.

There would be four ball boys patrolling each touchline and two bags of balls so there was an instant supply when the ball was kicked deep into the crowd. There were many more lineouts per game in those days and it was a way of keeping the tempo of the game high and to maximise the benefit of all Cov's superior fitness. Cov didn't want bulkier opposition forwards getting a decent breather while the ball took its time to reappear.

But what really strikes me now, nearly 50 years on, is how few of those concerned went on to win a significant number of caps and that's not a criticism. During this period Coventry were unquestionably the best team in the land but England, often poorly served by their selectors, somehow failed to harness the full power and potential of the club. But why would that be?

Perhaps the selectors were guilty of falling between two stalls. There was a marked reluctance to pick them en bloc or at least base the England team around them – the other clubs would surely be up in arms – so what tended to happen is that every time England failed or the selectors dithered or ran out of ideas they called up another couple of Cov players.

Cov were the best team in the land, and that would surely pay off in the end. Wouldn't it? Then, impatiently, England would ditch them pdq when there wasn't an instant upturn in results

So let's quickly go through the line-up, left to right: There is Bill Gittings, hard as nails scrum-half, with just one cap against New Zealand in 1973. Surely he was worth more than that but England were so erratic in their selections back then. Remember Bill was only playing against New Zealand because Jan Webster – England's MOM that summer of 73 when they beat the All Blacks in New Zealand – had somehow fallen from grace. Selection was Russian roulette.

Peter Preece, electric outside centre with the best outside break in the business, highly rated by the Welsh, should have won 40 caps not 12. Preece was a favourite player of mine and at the time I thought he was nailed on for the 1974 Lions where he would surely have caused

191

carnage on those hard grounds. It wasn't to be although I can't remember if he simply wasn't selected or if there were injury or availability issues.

Next comes Alan 'Dick' Cowman" talented fly-half who helped the North West beat the All Blacks in 1972 who had to make do with just five caps. He was another of the Loughborough University crew but another who suffered with the England merry-go-round, especially at ten, in the 70s.

Centre Geoff Evans, explosive off the mark, a 1974 Lion but restricted to nine England caps. One random titbit I always recalled from reading the England programmes of this era is that Evans was a former England schools Triple Jump champion. I certainly recall a proper athlete right down to the dodgy hamstrings of the highly tuned elite performer!

Roger Creed, utility forward one England cap v Rest of the World in 1971, good tough customer, while there is no need to elaborate on David Duckham. Full justice will be done to the great man elsewhere in this book but to this day I don't believe there has been a more glamorous England rugby player. He would be box office these days hounded by the top French clubs to play for them and fill their stadia.

Then we have the aforementioned Fairbrother and excellent mobile all-purpose prop and club stalwart who won 12 caps. Chris Wardlow was a tough ball carrier in midfield who won five caps.

The recently deceased John Barton was a terrific all round athlete who won five caps at lock. He would probably be a backrower these days and has to be one of the unluckiest of England players. In his youth, raw-boned and athletic, he broke into the England team in 1967 and went very well in his first two games – an 8-3 win over Ireland in Dublin and a narrow 16-12 defeat against France at Twickenham.

Then came England's end of season visit to Cardiff when Barton again impressed, indeed he scored two of England's three tries, one of them a cracker after good work from John Finlan and Budge Rogers.

Alas for him and England, the Welsh with Keith Jarrett to the fore, were inspired after the break and eventually ran out 34-21 winners.

Along with more than half the England team, Barton was banished from international rugby at the start of the following season and was totally ignored for five years when in 1972 it would appear nobody much fancied the trip to Paris and he was sensationally recalled to duty. England were massacred 37-12 and that signalled the end of his England career.

Peter Rossborough exciting attacking full-back and sevens specialist but only seven caps. He did though make an impressive 368 appearances for the club. Another Cov star never to be given a proper run. Barry Ninnes, tough durable lock who won one cap in 1971 against Wales. He logged 348 appearances for Cov

It is nonetheless a mighty line up especially given the two England fifteens caps who missed out and two other players of note

The one and only Fran Cotton was away resting after the England tour of New Zealand that summer, wing Rodney Webb – consistently under-appreciated by England – was also on his hols. "That fella Webb would run through a barn door if you asked him" was one of the earliest Bill McLaren lines I recall.

We should also mention Cov's No 8 around this time, Ron Jones who won five caps at No 8 for Wales 1967 and 1968 who for obvious reasons did not qualify for this picture.

Jones got unlucky, he had done pretty well in his first 12 months or so with Wales and played in that 37-21 win over England when Keith Jarrett took centre stage but alas for him Mervyn Davies was just beginning to get the taste for big match rugby. Jones was replaced by Davies at the start of the 1969 Five Nations and was, sadly for him, surplus to requirements thereafter. With Davies around most people would be.

Finally we must factor in Gray who, having starred for the England Seven that won the world invitation tournament at Murrayfield a few months earlier, had just turned professional with Wigan. There are those who insist that Gray – a cult figure when he played League in Australia – was the best English player never to win a full cap and I for one wouldn't disagree. He was a force of nature and Fran Cotton tells me he broke every known record in the gym and weights room at Loughborough where even the Olympic athletes couldn't live with him.

He was a cracking cricketer to boot and a round the corner goal kicker as well as a hooker. Leicester's Peter Wheeler, as he will tell you himself, was extremely grateful when Gray went north leaving the way clear for Peter's very considerable England career.

Brendan Gallagher

Majestic Cov

Players' Records

The following tables were kindly prepared by John Butler. The early entries date back to the Second World War and have been assembled from a variety of sources such as old programmes and newspaper articles, where club records no longer exist.

Many of the club's history and records were lost when Coundon Road was bombed. The records end in 2000, five years after the start of the professional era.

It is regretful that there are so many gaps in the early records and we hope that one of the results of publishing this book is that people will come forward and some of these will get filled.

FIRST NAME	LAST NAME	POSITION	FIRST SEASON	LAST SEASON	APPEARANCES	TRIES / POINTS (if known)	REPRESENTATIVE HONOURS & NOTES
Harold	Wheatley	Lock	1930/31	1947/48	26 post war		England, Barbarians, Midlands, Warks, CFC(RU) Club Captain
Herbert 'Neb'	Wheatley	Lock	1932/33	1946/47	2 post war		Midlands, Warwickshire
John	Kaye	Wing	1933/34	1948/49	1 post war	100 tries	Warwickshire
Harry	Pateman	Full back	1935/36	1949/50	100		Midlands, Warwickshire
Frank	Walton	Flanker	1937/38	1949/50	93	71 tries	Warwickshire
Norman	Stock	Scrum half	1938/39	1951/52	178		Midlands, Warwickshire
Gwyn	Davies	Full back	1939/40	1946/47	9		Warwickshire, Cambridge Blue, Two spells at CFC(RU)
Harold	Greasley	Wing	1939/40	1956/57	250 post war	181 tries overall	Midlands, Warwickshire, debut 15yrs 2mth Feb 1940
Wal	Gregory	Forward	1939/40	1948/49	57 post war		Warwickshire
J	Carpenter	Three-quarter	1942/43	1946/47	3		
Eric	Wright	Centre	1943/44	1948/49	62 post war	536 points overall	
J	Sparkes	Three-quarter	1944/45	1948/49	20	30 points post war	Warwickshire
Robert 'Bob'	Tilbury	Prop	1944/45	1948/49	32		Warwickshire
Eric	Ambler	Forward	1945/46	1948/49	8 post war		
D C	Powell	Forward	1945/46	1946/47	9		
Stan	Adkins	Lock	1946/47	1954/55	218		Midlands, Barbarians, Warwickshire
Ray	Batstone	Flanker	1946/47	1959/60	424	46 tries / 138 points	England trial, Midlands, Warwickshire
G	Cook	Three-quarter	1946/47	1946/47	3		
Bernard	Daniels	Forward	1946/47	1948/49	7 post war		
L M	Dodson	Three-quarter	1946/47	1946/47	2		
Roger	Draper	Three-quarter	1946/47	1949/50	19		
R	Ellis	Forward	1946/47	1946/47	4		
R	Gill	Forward	1946/47	1946/47	1		
P T	Mansell	Three-quarter	1946/47	1948/49	21		Warwickshire
D	Murray	Forward	1946/47	1946/47	1		
G B	Pears	Three-quarter	1946/47	1946/47	4		
Ivor	Preece	Fly half	1946/47	1955/56	135	135 tries	Lions, England, Barbarians, Midlands, Warwickshire
Ivor	Robinson	Hooker	1946/47	1954/55	38		Warwickshire
Harold	Smith	Centre	1946/47	1948/49	78 post war	130 points post war	Warwickshire
Roger	Spikes	Forward	1946/47	1949/50	7		
Don	Sproul	Fly half	1946/47	1946/47	7		Warwickshire
R	Taylor	Three-quarter	1946/47	1946/47	1		

FIRST NAME	LAST NAME	POSITION	FIRST SEASON	LAST SEASON	APPEARANCES	TRIES / POINTS (if known)	REPRESENTATIVE HONOURS & NOTES
J	Winship	Forward	1946/47	1946/47	1		
W G	Davies		1947/48	1947/48	4		Warwickshire
M	Dodd	Three-quarter	1947/48	1947/48	3		
R	Falkner	Forward	1947/48	1950/51	41		Warwickshire
J R	Fisher	Forward	1947/48	1947/48	3		
Stan	Graham	Flanker	1947/48	1953/54	54		Warwickshire
Wilf	Graham	Flanker / Full back	1947/48	1956/57	145		Warwickshire
John	Halford	Scrum / Fly half	1947/48	1950/51	33		Warwickshire
J	Henry	Forward	1947/48	1947/48	1		
A R	Hill	Forward	1947/48	1947/48	5		
Norman	Jones	Lock	1947/48	1054/55	138		Warwickshire
Bill	Ling	Centre	1947/48	1949/50	30		
John	Mauchlen	Wing	1947/48	1953/54	91	37 tries	Warwickshire
Eric	Roe	Three-quarter	1947/48	1947/48	24		Warwickshire
Alf	Sutton	Wing	1947/48	1956/57	116		Warwickshire
G A	Thompson	Three-quarter	1947/48	1947/48	4		
Harry	Walker	Prop	1947/48	1950/51	129		England, Barbarians, Mids, Warks, CFC(RU) & Warks President
G M	Wilkes	Three-quarter	1947/48	1947/48	7		
Tom	Windridge	Forward	1947/48	1947/48	34		Warwickshire
S J	Buttriss	Full back	1948/49	1948/49	1		
Frank	Castle	Wing	1948/49	1948/49	14	10 tries	Warwickshire
Charlie	Dupenois	Centre	1948/49	1951/52	82	24 points	Warwickshire
R	Ellis	Three-quarter	1948/49	1949/50	5		
Ted	Hewitt	Full back	1948/49	1953/54	138	252 points	England, Warwickshire
A	Johnson	Three-quarter	1948/49	1948/49	1		
J	Kennedy	Forward	1948/49	1948/49	2		
C	Norris	Three-quarter	1948/49	1948/49	2		
Neil	Parker	Wing	1948/49	1948/49	12		
Bob	Tilbury	Forward	Late war time	1948/49	24 post war		Warwickshire
George	Turnbull	Prop	1948/49	1958/59	167		Warwickshire
W G	Watson	Forward	1948/49	1948/49	6		Warwickshire
David	Butler	Lock	1949/50	1949/50	2		

FIRST NAME	LAST NAME	POSITION	FIRST SEASON	LAST SEASON	APPEARANCES	TRIES / POINTS (if known)	REPRESENTATIVE HONOURS & NOTES
John	Clifford	Winger	1949/50	1949/50	4		
Cliff	Everett	Full back	1949/50	1950/51	9		
John	Gardiner	No. 8	1949/50	1963/64	448	107 tries	England Trial, Barbarians, Mids, Warks, CFC(RU) Groundsman
S	Gough	Three-quarter	1949/50	1949/50	2		
David	Graham	Flanker	1949/50	1950/51	23		
Alan	Griffiths	Three-quarter	1949/50	1949/50	16		Warwickshire, Welsh trialist
J	James	Three-quarter	1949/50	1949/50	4		
David	Naylor	Flanker	1949/50	1952/53	88		RAF, Midlands, Warwickshire
Neil	Parker		1949/50	1949/50	28		Warwickshire
Marcus	Pearce	Wing	1949/50	1949/50	26	51 points	Warwickshire
Don	Roberts	Lock	1949/50	1960/61	78		Warwickshire
Ernie	Robinson	Hooker	1949/50	1961/62	321		England, Midlands, Warks, CFC(RU) Club Captain & Selector
	White		1949/50	1949/50	1		
Eric	Blackburn	Hooker	1950/51	1953/54	30		Lost a leg at Carbodies accident
B J	Clarke	Centre / Wing	1950/51	1952/53	41		
	Davidson		1950/51	1950/51	38		
David	Heath	Flanker	1950/51	1954/55	172		
Ryland	Jenkins	Scrum half	1950/51	1955/56	36		
Peter	Mottram	Full back	1950/51	1952/53	30	80 points	
	Roith		1950/51	1950/51	6		
Brian	Tomkins	Centre / Wing	1950/51	1952/53	61	213 points	Warwickshire
Max	Watson	Wing	1950/51	1954/55	24		
David	Baugh	Back	1951/52	1951/52	1		
Basil	Lilley	Prop	1951/52	1955/56	79		Warwickshire
Geoff	Long	Back	1951/52	1954/55	6		
J	Matthews		1951/52	1951/52	3		
J	Morris		1951/52	1952/53	7		
Brian 'Spike'	O'Donnell	Lock	1951/52	1955/56	109		Irish Trial, Warwickshire
David	Palmer	Centre	1951/52	1952/53	58	24 points	Leicestershire
Ivor	Robinson	Hooker	1951/52	1951/52	5		Warwickshire
Roy	Rowland	Fly half	1951/52	1952/53	22		
Jim	Stewart	Centre	1951/52	1958/59	128		Midlands, Warwickshire

Players' Records

FIRST NAME	LAST NAME	POSITION	FIRST SEASON	LAST SEASON	APPEARANCES	TRIES / POINTS (if known)	REPRESENTATIVE HONOURS & NOTES
Clem	Thomas	Flanker	1951/52	1952/53	18		Wales – whilst at CFC(RU)
Derrick	Ashcroft	Scrum half	1952/53	1953/54	46		Warwickshire
John	Butt	Scrum half	1952/53	1958/59	8		
Ian	Campbell	Fly half	1952/53	1953/54	17		Warwickshire
	Edwards		1952/53	1952/53	8		
Dick	Hollick	Lock	1952/53	1955/56	17		
Phil	Judd	Prop	1952/53	1967/68	442		England Barbarians, Mids, Warks, England & CFC(RU) Captain
Trevor	Meakin	Lock	1952/53	1956/57	68		Warwickshire
Peter	Robbins	Flanker	1952/53	1964/65	101		England, Barbarians, Midlands, Warwickshire, Oxford Blue
Stuart	Sanders	Fly half / Full back	1952/53	1960/61	162		Warwickshire
Derek	Trethaway	Wing	1952/53	1955/56	8		
Tony	Vyvyan	Centre	1952/53	1953/54	27		Warwickshire
John	Bluck	Wing	1953/54	1954/55	10		
Brian	Brighton	Centre	1953/54	1957/58	129		Notts Lincs & Derby
George	Cole	Scrum half	1953/54	1972/73	452 (club rec.)	2,858 points (club rec.)	Barbarians, Midlands, Warwickshire, CFC(RU) Club Captain
Alan	Davies	Centre	1953/54	1964/65	231		Warwickshire
Malcolm	Giles	Scrum half	1953/54	1953/54	1		
Peter	Jackson	Wing	1953/54	1962/63	186	127 tries	Lion. Midlands, Warwickshire, CFC(RU) Club Captain – Secretary
J	Robertson		1953/54	1953/54	2		
Bryan	Saville	Full back	1953/54	1955/56	34		
J	Stinchcombe		1953/54	1953/54	1		
Fenwick	Allison	Full back	1954/55	1957/58	64		England, Barbarians, Midlands, Warwickshire
Niall	Bailey	Wing	1954/55	1956/57	34		Ireland (whilst at Northampton)
David	Dove	Lock	1954/55	1962/63	64		Warwickshire
Bert	Godwin	Hooker	1954/55	1967/68	266		Lions, England, Barbarians, Midlandlands, Warwickshire
George	Grace	Prop	1954/55	1963/64	113		Warwickshire
J H 'Chick'	Henderson	Flanker	1954/55	1956/57	74		Scotland
Brian	Irvine	Fly half	1954/55	1959/60	55		Schools International, Warwickshire
Mike	McLean	Prop	1954/55	1963/64	285		Scottish trial, Midlands, Warwickshire
Terry	Pugh	Centre	1954/55	1955/56	5		
Tom	Reakes	Centre	1954/55	1955/56	15		
J S 'Ian'	Swan	Wing	1954/55	1956/57	55	28 tries	Scotland

Majestic Cov

FIRST NAME	LAST NAME	POSITION	FIRST SEASON	LAST SEASON	APPEARANCES	TRIES / POINTS (if known)	REPRESENTATIVE HONOURS & NOTES
Keith	Brookes	Flanker	1955/56	1962/63	83		Warwickshire
Lewis	Cannell	Centre	1955/56	1955/56	1		England
Mick	Hutt	No. 8	1955/56	1956/57	20		Warwickshire
E	King		1955/56	1955/56	1		
Derek	Ashurst	Flanker	1956/57	1957/58	10		
L R 'Bomber'	Evans	Flanker	1956/57	1966/67	205		RAF, Warwickshire
D	Gatfield		1956/57	1956/57	1		
D	Gilbert		1956/57	1956/57	1		
G	Hornsby		1956/57	1956/57	4		
John	Huins	Wing	1956/57	1958/59	54		
Ricky	Melville	Wing	1956/57	1968/69	386	281 tries (club rec.)	Midlands, Warwickshire
John	Moffitt	Centre	1956/57	1958/59	50		
G	Morris		1956/57	1956/57	1		
Terry	Pearson	Scrum half	1956/57	1957/58	17		
Brian	Porter	Full back	1956/57	1958/59	14		
John	Price	Lock	1956/57	1960/61	141		England, Warwickshire
B	Richards		1956/57	1956/57	1		
Graham	Watson	Back	1956/57	1961/62	27		
Nigel	White	Flanker	1956/57	1960/61	72		
Rob	Wilson	Full back	1956/57	1957/58	12		Oxford Blue, Warwickshire
D	Atherton		1957/58	1957/58	1		
John	Coates	Full back	1957/58	1959/60	32		Warwickshire
Ken	Freeborn	Wing	1957/58	1957/58	1		Midland Counties
D	Harrison		1957/58	1958/59	3		
Brian	Lavelle	Centre	1957/58	1958/59	7		
B	Moredike	Wing	1957/58	1958/59	5		
Goronwy	Morgan	Scrum half	1957/58	1959/60	53		
Peter	Morris	Centre	1957/58	1964/65	24		Warwickshire
S	Sutton		1957/58	1957/58	1		
Rogel	Abel	Centre	1958/59	1961/62	18		
John	Clamp	Prop	1958/59	1959/60	3		
Don	Clifton		1958/59	1958/59	1		

FIRST NAME	LAST NAME	POSITION	FIRST SEASON	LAST SEASON	APPEARANCES	TRIES / POINTS (if known)	REPRESENTATIVE HONOURS & NOTES
David	Cook	Full back	1958/59	1963/64	141		Warwickshire
Mick	Cook	Wing	1958/59	1958/59	1		
Doug	Curry	Wing	1958/59	1958/59	1		
Phil	Hall	Lock	1958/59	1967/68	72		Warwickshire
J	Harvey		1958/59	1958/59	21		
Mick	Lawrence	Flanker	1958/59	1961/62	26		
Kevin	Mountford	Flanker	1958/59	1959/60	23		
Tony	Pargetter	Centre	1958/59	1958/59	1		Warwickshire
Don	Sheward	Lock	1958/59	1958/59	1		
Dick	Webb	Wing	1958/59	1960/61	63		Warwickshire
Howard	Wyman	Hooker	1958/59	1970/71	171		Warwickshire
Bob	Barlow	Wing	1959/60	1963/64	11		
Bob	Frame	Centre	1959/60	1970/71	190		Midlands, Warwickshire
Tony	Green	Fly half	1959/60	1959/60	8		
Colin	Hewitt	Fly half	1959/60	1959/60	2		Warwickshire
Tony	Holt	Full back	1959/60	1969/70	143		Midlands, Warwickshire
Bob	Knott	Prop	1959/60	1973/74	239		Warwickshire
Harry	Knox	Centre	1959/60	1959/60	15		
Brian	Reade	Lock	1959/60	1961/62	8		
John	Shurvington	Centre	1959/60	1959/60	4		
John	Simmons		1959/60	1959/60	3		
Tim	Dalton	Fly half	1960/61	1968/69	249		England 1st replacement, Midlands, Warwickshire
Bob	Gaskell	Flanker	1960/61	1961/62	36		
Malcolm	Giles	Scrum half	1960/61	1960/61	1		
Neil	Kilpatrick	Full back	1960/61	1962/63	9		
Ralph	Lavelle	Centre	1960/61	1960/61	2		
Donald	Mackenzie	Forward	1960/61	1960/61	8		
Sam	Moore	Flanker	1960/61	1961/62	8		
Mick	Neale	Wing	1960/61	1962/63	34		Warwickshire
Jim	Wale	Winger	1960/61	1960/61	3		
D	Williams	Forward	1960/61	1960/61	1		
Dick	Andrews	Flanker	1961/62	1963/64	86		Warwickshire

FIRST NAME	LAST NAME	POSITION	FIRST SEASON	LAST SEASON	APPEARANCES	TRIES / POINTS (if known)	REPRESENTATIVE HONOURS & NOTES
John	Barton	Lock & No. 8	1961/62	1974/75	265		England, Barbarians, Midlands, Warwickshire
Jim	Broderick	Lock / Prop	1961/62	1979/80	385	40 tries	England to Japan, Babarians, Midlands, Warwickshire
Sid	Cooke	Flanker	1961/62	1962/63	7		
Peter	Courtois	Full back	1961/62	1962/63	6		
Colin	Fairbrother	Prop	1961/62	1961/62	8		Warwickshire
Rod	Gale	Forward	1961/62	1961/62	1		
Bob	Griffiths	Centre	1961/62	1971/72	162		Midlands, Warwickshire
John	Harrison		1961/62	1962/63	10		
Chris	Holmes	Flanker	1961/62	1974/75	140		Warwickshire
Duncan	Jenkins	Scrum half	1961/62	1963/64	9		
Peter	Morecombe	Wing	1961/62	1963/64	3		
Tom	Pargetter	Lock	1961/62	1962/63	31		England, Warwickshire
W	Prosser		1961/62	1961/62	1		
Pat	Smith	Wing	1961/62	1966/67	62		
Ken	Taylor	Full back	1961/62	1961/62	1		
C	Collins	Forward	1962/63	1963/64	2		
Jim	Flanagan	Wing	1962/63	1965/66	36		Warwickshire
David	Jenkins	Centre	1962/63	1967/68	50		Warwickshire
Roger	Millward	Lock	1962/63	1963/64	31		
John	Owen	Lock	1962/63	1967/68	156		England, Barbarians, Midlands, Warwickshire
Chris	Wheatley	Centre	1962/63	1973/74	297		Warwickshire
Brian	Wightman	No. 8	1962/63	1962/63	20		England
John	Finlan	Fly half	1963/64	1963/64	5		England – whilst at Moseley
Dick	Greenwood	Flanker	1963/64	1963/64	2		England – whilst at Waterloo
Freddie	Griffiths	Fly half	1963/64	1963/64	1		
D	Lindsay		1963/64	1963/64	1		
Cliff	Parrish	Flanker	1963/64	1966/67	63		North Midlands
Bill	Patterson	Centre	1963/64	1963/64	1		England
Harry	Prosser	Lock	1963/64	1970/71	144		Midlands, Warwickshire
J E	Roberts		1963/64	1963/64	1		
Mick	Stone		1963/64	1963/64	3		
Richard	Walker	Flanker	1963/64	1978/79	168	19 tries	Warwickshire

Players' Records

FIRST NAME	LAST NAME	POSITION	FIRST SEASON	LAST SEASON	APPEARANCES	TRIES / POINTS (if known)	REPRESENTATIVE HONOURS & NOTES
Rodney	Webb	Wing	1963/64	1973/74	165	118 tries	England, Barbarians, Midlands, Warwickshire
Dick	Andrews	Flanker	1964/65	1969/70	50		Warwickshire
Keith	Baughan	Hooker	1964/65	1965/66	9		
Peter	Carnall	Wing	1964/65	1965/66	26		
Gordon	Cresswell	Lock	1964/65	1964/65	6		
Tony	Davis	Scrum half	1964/65	1964/65	3		
Derek	Everest	Fly half	1964/65	1966/67	12		Warwickshire
Keith	Fairbrother	Prop	1964/65	1974/75	229		England, Barbarians, Midlands, Warwickshire, CFC(RU) Chairman
Bill	Gittings	Scrum half	1964/65	1976/77	317		England, Midlands, Warwickshire
Doug	Hill	Centre	1964/65	1964/65	1		
Les	Johnson	Full back	1964/65	1964/65	2		
Ron	Millward	Lock	1964/65	1965/66	13		
Jim	Moore	Back	1964/65	1964/65	2		
Dennis	Moore	Flanker	1964/65	1966/67	12		
Charlie	Mullen	Prop	1964/65	1965/66	4		
Ray	Phillips	Flanker	1964/65	1968/69	118		Cambridge Blue, North Midlands
Ron	Walker	Full back	1964/65	1965/66	41		Oxford Blue
Alan	Fisher	Centre	1965/66	1965/66	2		
Martin	Green	Flanker	1965/66	1965/66	1		
Pete	McConkey	Prop	1965/66	1966/67	55		Barbarians, Midlands, Staffordshire
Les	Rolinson	No. 8	1965/66	1972/73	181		
David	Scannell	Wing	1965/66	1967/68	10		
Ralph	Warmington	Wing	1965/66	1968/69	8		
Roger	Creed	Flanker	1966/67	1973/74	200		England, Warwickshire
David	Duckham	Centre / Wing	1966/67	1978/79	239	147 tries	Lions, England, Barbarians, Midlands, Warwickshire
Alan	James	Fly half	1966/67	1967/68	55		Midlands, Warwickshire
Howard	Jeffrey	Wing	1966/67	1966/67	1		
Ron	Jones	Flanker	1966/67	1972/73	107		
Malcolm	Lewis	Full back	1966/67	1966/67	2		Wales, Warwickshire
Malcolm	Stretton	Wing	1966/67	1966/67	10		Went on to become a successful coach
S	Taylor	Wing	1966/67	1967/68	3		
Roger	Warmington	Wing	1966/67	1967/68	73		

FIRST NAME	LAST NAME	POSITION	FIRST SEASON	LAST SEASON	APPEARANCES	TRIES / POINTS (if known)	REPRESENTATIVE HONOURS & NOTES
Gordon	Baggott	Scrum half	1967/68	1967/68	4		
Eddie	Calcott	Full back	1967/68	1967/68	20		
Malcolm	Edwards	Forward	1967/68	1967/68	3		Warwickshire
John	Hofton	Wing	1967/68	1967/68	4		
Colin	Jeffries	Wing	1967/68	1967/68	4		
Peter	Jordan	Flanker	1967/68	1971/72	30		Warwickshire
John	Lacey	Lock	1967/68	1969/70	18		Warwickshire
David	Nicholls	Fly half	1967/68	1974/75	137		Warwickshire
Peter	Rossborough	Full back	1967/68	1981/82	368	109 tries / 2,052 points	England, Barbarians, Midlands, Warwickshire
J G A	Warren	Forward	1967/68	1968/69	4		Midlands, Warwickshire
Mike	Barnwell	Scrum half	1968/69	1973/74	11		Warwickshire
J P 'Nobby'	Bolton	Wing	1968/69	1973/74	179	122 tries	Midlands, Warwickshire
David	Cook	Wing	1968/69	1974/75	36		Warwickshire
Graham	Creed	Prop	1968/69	1973/74	102		Midlands, Warwickshire
Ian	Darnell	Lock	1968/69	1978/79	290	22 tries	Warwickshire
John	Gallagher	Hooker	1968/69	1975/76	177		Warwickshire
Brian	Holt	Flanker	1968/69	1977/78	177	27 tries	Warwickshire
Chris	Lea	Full back	1968/69	1969/70	5		Warwickshire
Jim	Moore		1968/69	1968/69	1		
Peter	Preece	Centre / Wing	1968/69	1977/78	183	104 tries	England, Barbarians, Midlands, Warwickshire
John	Rolfe	Wing	1968/69	1972/73	18		
Derek	Simpson	Lock	1968/69	1976/77	129	12 tries	Warwickshire
Maurice	Campton	Wing	1969/70	1973/74	72		Warwickshire
Geoff	Evans	Centre	1969/70	1982/83	174	71 tries	Lions, Barbarians, Midlands, Warwickshire
	Harris		1969/70	1969/70	21		
Barry	Ninnes	Lock	1969/70	1980/81	348	34 tries	England, Midlands, Warwickshire
G	Owen	Centre	1969/70	1969/70	1		
Paul	Bryan	No. 8	1970/71	1976/77	137		Warwickshire
Bernard	Capaldi	Flanker	1970/71	1971/72	39		
Chris	Gifford	Scrum half	1970/71	1975/76	68		North Midlands
John	Gray	Hooker	1970/71	1972/73	51		Barbarians, Midlands, Warwick
M	Griffiths		1970/71	1970/71	1		

Players' Records

FIRST NAME	LAST NAME	POSITION	FIRST SEASON	LAST SEASON	APPEARANCES	TRIES / POINTS (if known)	REPRESENTATIVE HONOURS & NOTES
	Hemmings		1970/71	1971/72	2		
	Kilborn		1970/71	1970/71	1		
	Morgan		1970/71	1970/71	1		
	Parkin		1970/71	1970/71	1		
Steve	Adams	Full back	1971/72	1973/74	18		Warwickshire
Alan	Cowman	Fly half	1971/72	1978/79	160	27 tries	England, North
Alastair	Jameson	Prop	1971/72	1972/73	4		
	Parkin		1971/72	1971/72	2		
Tim	Barnwell	Wing	1972/73	1976/77	80		Brother of Mike
Barrie	Corless	Centre	1972/73	1975/76	95		England, North Midlands
Paul	Coulthard	Centre	1972/73	1979/80	183	27 tries	Warwickshire
J	Cusack		1972/73	1972/73	1		
M	Fenlon		1972/73	1972/73	1		
P	Galloway		1972/73	1972/73	1		
John	Handley	Forward	1972/73	1974/75	4		
A	Moore		1972/73	1972/73	1		
Bob	Timothy	Hooker	1972/73	1975/76	11		
Alf	Troughton	Lock	1972/73	1975/76	29		
Chris	Wardlow	Centre	1972/73	1974/75	46		England, Barbarians, North
J	Wilson		1972/73	1972/73	1		
Miles	Barker-Davies	Hooker	1973/74	1976/77	22		Son of former Club Chairman, Jack
Steve	Brown	Forward	1973/74	1977/78	7		
Robin	Cardwell	Flanker	1973/74	1978/79	98	7 tries	Warwickshire
Fran	Cotton	Prop	1973/74	1974/75	20		British Lion – not whilst at CFC(RU), England – whilst at CFC(RU)
Malcolm	Edwards	Prop	1973/74	1973/74	6		
Paul	Evans	Full back	1973/74	1978/79	71	9 tries	Warwickshire
J	Falkner		1973/74	1973/64	2		
David	Foulks	Centre	1973/74	1982/83	127	20 tries	Warwickshire
Colin	Grimshaw	Scrum half	1973/74	1979/80	127	29 tries	Ireland – not whilst at CFC(RU)
Russ	Knee	Wing	1973/74	1981/82	60	11 tries	Warwickshire
Mark	Lookman	Lock	1973/74	1973/74	7		
Simon	Maisey	Wing	1973/74	1983/84	252	110 tries / 435 points	Warwickshire, England Schools, U23, Trialist

Majestic Cov

FIRST NAME	LAST NAME	POSITION	FIRST SEASON	LAST SEASON	APPEARANCES	TRIES / POINTS (if known)	REPRESENTATIVE HONOURS & NOTES
Mal	Malik	Flanker	1973/74	1985/86	179	41 tries	Warwickshire
Stewart	Martin	Full back	1973/74	1974/75	28		Warwickshire
Roy	Pebody	Fly half / Centre	1973/74	1973/74	2		
D	Quinney	Forward	1973/74	1973/74	6		Club coach for short time
Jim	Robinson	Prop	1973/74	1975/76	30		
Ken	Sheerman	Forward	1973/74	1973/74	1		Warwickshire
Les	Campbell	Prop	1974/75	1980/81	51		
Lindsay	Carver	Flanker	1974/75	1974/75	1		
Martin	Clifford	Wing	1974/75	1983/84	80	13 tries	Warwickshire
Trevor	Corless	Prop	1974/75	1975/76	55		Midlands, North Midlands
Adam	Dunning	Centre	1974/75	1975/76	6		
Richard	Hawthorne	Forward	1974/75	1974/75	1		
Brett	Kirton	Back	1974/75	1974/75	1		
Martyn	Osborne	Centre	1974/75	1979/80	18	5 tries	
J	Shaw		1974/75	1974/75	1		
Jon	Shipsides	Flanker	1974/75	1980/81	123	12 tries	Midlands, North Midlands
J	Wilson		1974/75	1977/78	3		
W	Wilson		1974/75	1974/75	1		
D	Bullock	Forward	1975/76	1975/76	1		
Brian	Clifford	Wing	1975/76	1975/76	1		
Thumper	Dingley	Prop	1975/76	1981/82	134	10 tries	Warwickshire
Rob	Fardoe	Lock	1975/76	1983/84	145	7 tries	Warwickshire
Steve	Hall	Full back	1975/76	1979/80	57	2 tries	Warwickshire
John	Hamer	Prop	1975/76	1977/78	62	2 tries	
Stuart	Hamilton	Centre	1975/76	1977/78	46	18 tries	
Rod	Hughes		1975/76	1975/76	1		
Paul	Knee	Wing	1975/76	1982/83	157	105 tries	Midlands, Warwickshire
Paul	Lander	Scrum half	1975/76	1983/84	106	36 tries	Warwickshire
Charlie	McCarthy	Lock	1975/76	1980/81	94	2 tries	
Fred	Melvin	Prop	1975/76	1980/81	85		Warwickshire
Steve	Oliver	Flanker	1975/76	1979/80	136	7 tries	Warwickshire
E	Oliver		1975/76	1975/76	1		

208

Players' Records

FIRST NAME	LAST NAME	POSITION	FIRST SEASON	LAST SEASON	APPEARANCES	TRIES / POINTS (if known)	REPRESENTATIVE HONOURS & NOTES
A	Partridge		1975/76	1975/76	1		
Mike	Sweeney	Forward	1975/76	1976/77	6		
Keith	Aitchison	Fly half	1976/77	1977/78	58	16 tries	North Midlands
Neville	Bakewell	Lock	1976/77	1978/79	45	1 try	
Terry	Bateman	Back	1976/77	1976/77	1		
Bernie	Clarke	Flanker	1976/77	1981/82	68	10 tries	
Andy	Farrington	Hooker	1976/77	1981/82	239	12 tries	Warwickshire
Lee	Johnson	Prop	1976/77	1989/90	268	57 tries	England, Midlands, Warwickshire
M	Johnson		1976/77	1976/77	1		
E	Mazurek	Forward	1976/77	1976/77	1		
Martin	Slagter	Lock	1976/77	1977/78	23	2 tries	
Keith	Tysall	Full back	1976/77	1976/77	7		
Caspar	Weston	Hooker	1976/77	1983/84	82	9 tries	
Les	Bend	Flanker	1977/78	1977/78	2		
Simon	Gregory	No. 8	1977/78	1980/81	22	4 tries	
John	Hecht	Prop	1977/78	1977/78	3		
Graham	Robbins	No. 8	1977/78	1989/90	263	118 tries	England, Babarians, Midlands, Warwickshire
Robin	Sadler	Flanker	1977/78	1983/84	116	9 tries	North Midlands
Garry	Watts	Wing	1977/78	1977/78	1		
Caspar	Weston	Hooker	1977/78	1983/84	82	9 tries	
Steve	Wilkes	Prop	1977/78	1991/92	366	5 tries	Midlands, Warwickshire
St J	Williamson	Lock	1977/78	1977/78	1		
Nigel	Wright	Fly half	1977/78	1983/84	43	21 points	Two spells
David	Bailey	Fly half / Centre	1978/79	1981/82	81	16 tries	
Mike	Scott	Flanker	1978/79	1980/81	8		
Mark	Woodhead	Centre / Wing	1978/79	1988/89	82	18 tries	Two spells at CFC(RU)
Steve	Brain	Hooker	1979/80	1983/84	185	13 tries	England, Warwickshire
Steve	Brown	Lock	1979/80	1979/80	17	2 tries	
Tim	Buttimore	Centre / Fly half	1979/80	1983/84	103	24 tries	
Huw	Davies	Fly half	1979/80	1982/83	89	23 tries	Warwickshire
Kim	Dodd	Flanker	1979/80	1981/82	23	1 try	England, Barbarians, Midlands
Roy	Freemantle	Hooker	1979/80	1984/85	12		

FIRST NAME	LAST NAME	POSITION	FIRST SEASON	LAST SEASON	APPEARANCES	TRIES / POINTS (if known)	REPRESENTATIVE HONOURS & NOTES
Roddy	Grant	Full back / Centre	1979/80	1984/85	26	9 tries	Two short spells at CFC(RU)
Tony	Gulliver	Lock	1979/80	1995/96	381	11 tries	Warwickshire
Ian	Stokes	Fly half	1979/80	1981/82	25	3 tries	
Steve	Thomas	Scrum half	1979/80	1992/93	310	76 tries	Midlands, Warwickshire
Huw	Bevan	Full back / Centre	1980/81	1984/85	56	55 points	Warwickshire
Jamie	Dodd	Flanker	1980/81	1981/82	3		
John	Eaton	Wing	1980/81	1982/83	29	9 tries	
Martin	Hobley	Prop	1980/81	1983/84	34		
Neil	Hudman	Centre	1980/81	1982/83	31	9 tries	
Chris	Ison	Centre / Fly half	1980/81	1981/82	13	4 tries	Warwickshire
Mark	Lakey	Fly half	1980/81	1994/95	200	325 points	Out of the game for 2 1/2 years with knee injury
Rob	Mauchlen	Fly half	1980/81	1982/83	4	2 tries	Son of John from the 1950s
Chris	Millerchip	Centre	1980/81	1987/88	51	14 points	Oxford Blue
Mel	Parnell	Flanker	1980/81	1982/83	22	3 tries	
Marcus	Rose	Full back	1980/81	1983/84	43	6 tries / 346 points	England, Barbarians, Midlands
Andy	Rymell	Lock	1980/81	1981/82	8		
Paul	Thomas	Flanker	1980/81	1995/96	280	62 tries	Warwickshire
Mark	Brooke	Wing / Centre	1981/82	1981/82	2		
Neil	Gutteridge	Hooker	1981/82	1983/84	9		
Tery	Hart	Lock	1981/82	1981/82	1		
Brian	Kidner	Lock	1981/82	1988/89	176	6 tries	Warwickshire
Mark	Ogilby	Lock	1981/82	1981/82	1		
Martin	Rawbone	Flanker	1981/82	1981/82	1		
Max	Reeve	Prop	1981/82	1982/83	8	1 try	
Graham	Rossborough	Fly half	1981/82	1981/82	3		
Russell	West	Scrum half	1981/82	1983/84	18	3 tries	
Russell	Whitworth	Wing	1981/82	1983/84	17	3 tries	
Paul	Bagnall	Centre	1982/83	1982/83	5		
Paul	Bowkett	Prop	1982/83	1982/83	2		
John	Cooke	Centre	1982/83	1985/86	73	19 tries	
Bob	Massey	Centre	1982/83	1985/86	74	73 points	Warwickshire
Andy	Rooke	No. 8	1982/83	1986/87	53	19 tries	

FIRST NAME	LAST NAME	POSITION	FIRST SEASON	LAST SEASON	APPEARANCES	TRIES / POINTS (if known)	REPRESENTATIVE HONOURS & NOTES
Chris	Royle	Wing	1982/83	1985/86	51	12 tries	
Jan	Webster	Scrum half	1982/83	1982/83	1		England – whilst at Moseley
Tim	Cooke	Fly half	1983/84	1983/84	1		
Paul	Edwards	Lock	1983/84	1983/84	1		
Steve	Elvidge	Hooker	1983/84	1985/86	7		
Martin	Fairn	Full back / Centre	1983/84	1991/92	239	821 points	Warwickshire
Martin	Fleetwood	Lock	1983/84	1985/86	16	1 try	
Mark	Ison	Lock	1983/84	1983/84	2		
W	Mousley	Flanker	1983/84	1983/84	1		
Eddie	Saunders	Wing	1983/84	1986/87	125	59 tries	North Midlands
Graham	Staley	Prop	1983/84	1984/85	15	3 tries	Staffordshire
Paul	Stringfellow	Scrum half	1983/84	1983/84	1		
Micky	Summers	Wing	1983/84	1984/85	60	21 tries	
Dick	Travers	Flanker	1983/84	1991/92	158	46 tries	Army, Warwickshire
Micky	Trumper	Flanker	1983/84	1987/88	77	8 tries	North Midlands
Bob	Watts	Scrum half	1983/84	1983/84	7	2 tries	
David	Clark	Scrum half	1984/85	1990/91	48	47 points	
Kevin	Clarke	Full back	1984/85	1984/85	1		
Stuart	Hall	Wing	1984/85	1990/91	171	62 tries	Warwickshire
Mick	Jones	Back	1984/85	1984/85	2		
Neil	Leeming	Flanker	1984/85	1984/85	2		
Charlie	Ralston	Centre / Full back	1984/85	1986/87	50	62 points	
Garry J	Smith	Prop	1984/85	1985/86	10		
Gary N	Smith	Centre	1984/85	1989/90	12		
Graham	Warrington	Lock	1984/85	1985/86	17	1 try	
Andy	Ambrose	No. 8	1985/86	1985/86	3		
Clive	Davies	Hooker	1985/86	1986/87	10		
Clive	Folwell	Flanker	1985/86	1985/86	3		
David	Jones	Centre	1985/86	1988/89	59	12 tries	
Craig	Langstone	Scrum half	1985/86	1986/87	11	1 try	
Clive	Meanwell	Full back	1985/86	1985/86	17	62 points	
Clive	Medford	Centre	1985/86	1991/92	146	12 tries	Warwickshire

FIRST NAME	LAST NAME	POSITION	FIRST SEASON	LAST SEASON	APPEARANCES	TRIES / POINTS (if known)	REPRESENTATIVE HONOURS & NOTES
Glyn	Owen	Centre	1985/86	1987/88	13	4 tries	Warwickshire
Trevor	Revan	Prop	1985/86	2002/03	106	10 tries	Policeman
Paul	Suckling	Flanker	1985/86	1989/90	54	14 tries	
Clive	Wynter	Wing	1985/86	1986/87	19	3 tries	
Mark	Bennett	Wing	1986/87	1992/93	47	8 tries	Warwickshire
Andy	Beveridge	Flanker	1986/87	1986/87	1		
Richard	Briggs	Wing	1986/87	1986/87	1		
Steve	Fairn	Flanker	1986/87	1990/91	29	4 tries	
Ken	Ferdinand	Flanker / No. 8	1986/87	1993/94	25	2 tries	
Steve	Freemantle	Hooker	1986/87	1986/87	1		
Julian	Hyde	Lock	1986/87	1996/97	213	5 tries	Warwickshire
Kent	James	Centre / Wing	1986/87	1988/89	28	1 try	
Keith	Jervis	Centre	1986/87	1986/87	14	1 try	
David	Kennell	Wing	1986/87	1986/87	4	1 try	
Mike	Llewellyn	Scrum half	1986/87	1986/87	1		
Russ	Mannix	Lock	1986/87	1988/89	12		
Jason	Minshull	Centre	1986/87	2000/01	220	32 tries	Two spells at CFC(RU) 1986 – 1993 & 1996 – 2001
Andy	Parton	Wing	1986/87	1992/93	80	19 tries	
Rob	Rowan	Fly half	1986/87	1992/93	76	120 points	
Peter	Rowland	Flanker	1986/87	1988/89	64	11 tries	
Andy	Savage	Scrum half	1986/87	1991/92	108	11 tries	Warwickshire
Chris	Sibley	Centre	1986/87	1987/88	11	2 tries	
Jez	Tiff	Wing	1986/87	1988/89	5		
Gareth	Tregilgas	Prop	1986/87	1996/97	162	8 tries	Warwickshire Club Captain
Terry	Williams	Flanker	1986/87	1986/87	7	1 try	
Mark	Wood	Full back	1986/87	1986/87	7	11 points	
Chris	Carvell	No. 8 / Flanker	1987/88	1987/88	4		
Gary	Colleran	Hooker	1987/88	1987/88	8		
D	Davies	Hooker	1987/88	1988/89	4		
Dave	Fowler-Simons	Prop	1987/88	1989/90	9		
Jim	Graham	Centre	1987/88	1988/89	50	8 tries	
Rob	Heggatt	Lock	1987/88	1987/88	7		

Players' Records

FIRST NAME	LAST NAME	POSITION	FIRST SEASON	LAST SEASON	APPEARANCES	TRIES / POINTS (if known)	REPRESENTATIVE HONOURS & NOTES
S	Holloway	No. 8	1987/88	1987/88	1	1 try	
C	James	Flanker	1987/88	1987/88	5		
S	Lanchbury	Lock	1987/88	1987/88	1		
Chris	Leake	Wing	1987/88	1987/88	13	5 tries	
Leroy	McKenzie	Wing	1987/88	1992/93	146	50 tries	Moved to RL
Steve	Miles	Scrum half	1987/88	1990/91	4		
Ian	Potter	Full back	1987/88	1987/88	13	67 points	
Paul	Quinlan	Flanker	1987/88	1988/89	8		
Andy	Roda	Prop	1987/88	1989/90	18		
Tim	Webb	Scrum half	1987/88	1987/88	1		
John	Williamson	Scrum half	1987/88	1988/89	6		
Steve	Wood	No. 8	1987/88	1987/88	5	1 try	
Simon	Wright	Flanker	1987/88	1988/89	34	2 tries	
Rob	Albertsma	Lock	1988/89	1988/89	1		
Karl	Barnfather	Flanker	1988/89	1988/89	6		
Paul	Barran	Flanker	1988/89	1988/89	1		
John	Brain	No. 8	1988/89	1989/90	14		
John	Cockerill	Centre	1988/89	1988/89	1		
Chris	Hall	Lock	1988/89	1988/89	19	2 tries	
Kevin	Hickey	Flanker	1988/89	1995/96	156	49 tries	North Midlands
Leyton	Jones	Centre	1988/89	1989/90	11		
Peter	McKenzie	Flanker	1988/89	1991/92	12		
Phil	Miles	Scrum half	1988/89	1994/95	9		
Simon	Reid	Full back	1988/89	1988/89	7	19 Points	
Gary	Sharp	Hooker	1988/89	1994/95	73	4 tries	
Steve	Smith	No. 8	1988/89	1990/91	50	2 tries	
Phil	Stone	Flanker	1988/89	1993/94	22		
Peter	Tandy	Wing	1988/89	1988/89	5	2 tries	
Gary	Wainwright	Fly half	1988/89	1988/89	1		
Mike	Wisheart	Wing	1988/89	1989/90	9	2 tries	
Dave	Addleton	Hooker	1989/90	2008/09	355	23 tries	
Dinos	Andreou	Lock	1989/90	1997/98	32	1 try	Irish Exiles, Babarians, Midlands, Warwickshire Forwards Coach

FIRST NAME	LAST NAME	POSITION	FIRST SEASON	LAST SEASON	APPEARANCES	TRIES / POINTS (if known)	REPRESENTATIVE HONOURS & NOTES
Steve	Chapman	Centre / Wing	1989/90	1996/97	125	102 points	Warwickshire
Rob	Cockerton	Lock	1989/90	1989/90	1		
Chris	Crang	Hooker	1989/90	1989/90	1		
Richard	Gee	Full back	1989/90	1996/97	95	122 points	Warwickshire
Rob	Hardwick	Prop	1989/90	1997/98	144	12 tries	England, Barbarians, Warwick
Richard	Mackie	Lock	1989/90	1994/95		41 points	
Warwick	Masser	Fly half / Centre	1989/90	1990/91	9	12 points	Warwickshire
Gareth	Mitchell	Fly half	1989/90	1993/94	10	40 points	
David	Morgan	Wing	1989/90	1994/95	8	1 try	
David	Paull	Flanker	1989/90	1989/90	13	2 tries	
Mark	Pearson	Flanker	1989/90	1991/92	22	1 try	
Ian	Pickup	No. 8	1989/90	1990/91	25	6 tries	
John	Russell	Centre	1989/90	1989/90	2		
Marc	Thomas	Full back	1989/90	1996/97	52	324 points	Warwickshire
Martin	Toombs	Fly half	1989/90	1989/90	5	2 tries	
Richard	Angell	Fly half	1990/91	1996/97	179	805 points	
Chris	Barbor	Hooker	1990/91	1990/91	2		
Stuart	Barden	Centre / Wing	1990/91	1996/97	58	39 poins	Warwickshire
Warwick	Bullock	Prop	1990/91	1997/98	122	13 points	Warwickshire
Richard	Cockerill	Hooker	1990/91	1991/92	27		First Captain Colts squad
Mark	Crees	Lock	1990/91	1990/91	4		
Neil	Pettipher	Prop	1990/91	1991/92	9		
Shayne	Philpott	Centre / Full back	1990/91	1990/91	9	17 points	New Zealand – not capped whilst at CFC(RU), Wakefield
Kevin	Shaw	Wing	1990/91	1992/93	13	3 tries	
Greg	Smith	Flanker	1990/91	1990/91	20	4 tries	
Peter	Butler	Prop	1991/92	1992/93	5	1 try	
Clint	Chadwick	Flanker	1991/92	1991/92	21	4 tries	
Craig	Cosgrove	No. 8	1991/92	1991/92	6	2 tries	
Roger	Crockford	No. 8	1991/92	1991/92	1		
Jim	Cross	Lock	1991/92	1991/92	2		
Jim	Darragh	Flanker	1991/92	1991/92	1		
Gavin	Dick	Wing	1991/92	1991/92	1		

FIRST NAME	LAST NAME	POSITION	FIRST SEASON	LAST SEASON	APPEARANCES	TRIES / POINTS (if known)	REPRESENTATIVE HONOURS & NOTES
Barrie	Evans	Wing	1991/92	1993/94	77	32 tries	
Rob	Field	Lock	1991/92	1993/04	48	3 tries	
Jason	Marvelly	Scrum half	1991/92	1991/92	1		
Rob	Masterson	Fly half	1991/92	1991/92	3		
Kevin	Street	Centre	1991/92	1992/93	9		
Barry	Sylvester	Scrum half	1991/92	1995/96	5		
Damion	Tabram	Prop	1991/92	1991/92	28		
Richard	Turner	Scrum half	1991/92	1992/93	44	13 points	
Nav	Uppal	Lock	1991/92	1991/92	1		
Stuart	Vaudin	Full back	1991/92	1991/92	1		
Dave	Butler	Scrum half	1992/93	1993/94	2		
Steve	Carter	No. 8 / Flanker	1992/93	1994/95	39	7 tries	
Gavin	Caswell	Flanker	1992/93	1994/95	11	2 tries	
Mick	Curtis	Centre	1992/93	2004/05	204	28 tries	Warwickshire
Mark	Douglas	Scrum half	1992/93	1994/95	26	17 tries	Wales – not capped whilst at CFC(RU)
Mark	Elvidge	Scrum half	1992/93	1992/93	1		
Chris	Gardner	Flanker	1992/93	1993/94	3		
Greg	Harwood	Fly half	1992/93	1992/93	12		
Lee	Jones	No. 8	1992/93	1992/93	13	1 try	
Crayton	Phillips	Prop	1992/93	1993/94	34	7 tries	
Ben	Shepherd	Wing	1992/93	1996/97	56	37 tries	Warwickshire
Nick	Stainton	Full back	1992/93	1992/93	1		
Peter	Staveley	Flanker	1992/93	1992/93	2		
Jim	Wingham	Prop	1992/93	1992/93	1		
Steve	Allen	Centre	1993/94	1995/96	5		
Gavin	Allinson	Flanker	1993/94	1996/97	22	2 tries	
Elliot	Blundell	Scrum half	1993/94	1994/95	20	12 points	
M	Brown	Centre	1993/94	1993/94	1		
Mike	Butler	Scrum half	1993/94	1993/94	2		Oxford Blue
Lee	Crofts	Flanker	1993/94	2003/04	247	45 tries	Warwickshire
Ian	Dee	Centre	1993/94	1993/95	1		
Simon	Dowson	Scrum half	1993/94	1994/95	39	3 tries	

FIRST NAME	LAST NAME	POSITION	FIRST SEASON	LAST SEASON	APPEARANCES	TRIES / POINTS (if known)	REPRESENTATIVE HONOURS & NOTES
Colin	Field	Centre	1993/94	1993/94	1		
Simon	Hancox	Hooker	1993/94	1995/96	49	12 tries	
Tim	Harrison		1993/94	1993/94	1		
Kevin	Herbert		1993/94	1993/94	1		
Julian	Horrobin	Flanker	1993/94	2002/03	249	74 tries	
Duncan	Keenan	Full back	1993/94	1994/95	4	3 tries	
S	Lloyd-Jones	Centre	1993/94	1993/94	1		
Rob	Merritt	Prop	1993/94	1993/94	1		
Rob	Merritt	Prop	1993/94	1993/94	1		
Willie	Phillips	No. 8	1993/94	1993/94	15	2 tries	
Ben	Powis	Wing	1993/94	1995/96	16	2 tries	Warwickshire
Craig	Quick	Full back	1993/94	1995/96	30	231 points	Warwickshire
Nick	Thomson	Centre	1993/94	1995/96	24	28 points	
Doug	Woodman	Wing	1993/94	1996/97	61	42 tries	Two spells – came back from Lydney
Tim	Woolman	Full back	1993/94	1993/94	3	1 try	
Tigger	Dawson	Scrum half	1994/95	2002/03	177	24 tries	
Nick	Dougill	Wing	1994/95	1994/95	3		
Alex	Gissing	Lock	1994/95	1994/95	7		
Danny	Grewcock	Lock	1994/95	1996/97	55	6 tries	England – after leaving CFC(RU)
Paul	Harrison	Fly half / Centre	1994/95	1994/95	7	8 points	
John	Hart	Centre / Fly half	1994/95	1997/98	50	95 points	
Nick	Lewis	Prop	1994/95	1996/97	27	1 try	
Russ	Morgan	Prop	1994/95	2001/02	48	3 tries	Warwickshire
James	Priestley	Hooker	1994/95	1994/95	3		
Eddie	Simkiss	Flanker	1994/95	1999/2000	8	2 tries	
Steve	Smith	No. 8	1994/95	1995/96	37	7 tries	
Gary	Talbot	Flanker	1994/95	1994/95	3		
Simon	Van Pelt		1994/95	1994/95	1		
Bernie	Williams	Prop	1994/95	1997/98	38	1 try	
Richard	Blundell	Hooker	1995/96	1996/97	12		
Lee	Clarke	Wing	1995/96	1996/97	2	2 tries	
Derek	Eves	Flanker	1995/96	1999/2000	103	23 tries	Player Coach, Director of Rugby

Players' Records

FIRST NAME	LAST NAME	POSITION	FIRST SEASON	LAST SEASON	APPEARANCES	TRIES / POINTS (if known)	REPRESENTATIVE HONOURS & NOTES
David	John	Wing	1995/96	1996/97	7	3 tries	
Paul	Lydster	Scrum half	1995/96	1997/98	33	17 tries	Warwickshire
Paul	Morgan	Centre / Wing	1995/96	1995/96	2	2 tries	
Pete	Nisbitt	Wing	1995/96	1995/96	1	1 try	
Ian	Patten	No. 8	1995/96	1997/98	63	12 tries	
Garrath	Reayer	Centre	1995/96	1997/98	27	9 tries	
Sam	Russell	Flanker	1995/96	1996/97	10	2 tries	
Alastair	Saverimutto	Centre	1995/96	1995/96	12	13 points	Brother of Robin
Robin	Saverimutto	Scrum half	1995/96	1995/96	13	3 tries	Brother of Alastair
Andy	Blackmore	Lock	1996/97	1997/98	45	5 tries	
James	Brown	Fly half	1996/97	1997/98	23	149 points	
Mark	Crane	Prop	1996/97	1998/99	51	5 tries	
John	Farr	Scrum half	1996/97	1997/98	13	5 tries	
Matt	Gallagher	Centre	1996/97	2000/01	100	17 tries / 205 points	
Jez	Harris	Fly half	1996/97	1997/98	46	500 points	Holds club league record for number of points in a game
Adam	Irwin	Wing	1996/97	1998/99	14	4 tries	
Wayne	Kilford	Full back	1996/97	1998/99	67	96 points	
Richard	Lloyd	Flanker	1996/97	1997/98	13	4 tries	
David	Lockley	Fly half	1996/97	1996/97	2	11 points	
Andy	McAdam	Wing	1996/97	1998/99	53	28 tries	
Richie	Robinson	Centre	1996/97	1998/99	71	20 tries	
Rob	Salisbury	Flanker	1996/97	1998/99	34	6 tries	
Alan	Sharp	Prop	1996/97	1998/99	36		Scotland – not whilst at CFC(RU)
Andy	Smallwood	Wing	1996/97	2000/01	127	66 tries	For many years held the club try scoring record by season
James	Soden	Hooker	1996/97	1998/99	21		
Glen	Southwell	Flanker	1996/97	1997/98	6	1 try	
David	Duley	Lock	1997/98	1997/98	21	2 tries	New Zealander
Simon	Edwards	No. 8	1997/98	1998/99	4		
Richard	Faiers	Prop	1997/98	1997/98	6		
Carl	Fripp	Lock	1997/98	1997/98	3		
Vince	Hartland	Lock	1997/98	1997/98	11		
Jason	Hewlett	Scrum half	1997/98	1998/99	17	2 tries	

FIRST NAME	LAST NAME	POSITION	FIRST SEASON	LAST SEASON	APPEARANCES	TRIES / POINTS (if known)	REPRESENTATIVE HONOURS & NOTES
Gareth	Jones	Wing	1997/98	1997/98	5	2 tries	
Ralph	Knibbs	Centre	1997/98	1997/98	1		
Ken	Stewart	No. 8	1997/98	1997/98	4		
Danny	Zaltzman	Lock	1997/98	1997/98	15		
Richard	Ayres	Prop	1998/99	1998/99	5		
James	Brierley	Wing	1998/99	1998/99			
James	Cathcart	Full back	1998/99	1999/2000	11	13 poins	
Luis	Criscuolo	Centre	1998/99	2002/03	38	39 points	Argentina – not whilst at CFC(RU)
B	Dale		1998/99	1998/99	1		
Mark	Fountaine	Prop	1998/99	1999/2000	56	4 tries	
Steve	Gough	Fly half	1998/99	1999/2000	55	624 points	Club league record at the time
James	Hadfield	Prop	1998/99	2002/03	27		
Chris	Houston	Flanker	1998/99	1998/99	10	1 try	
Ricky	Hyslop	Wing	1998/99	1999/2000	24	7 tries	
Steve	Kerr	Prop	1998/99	1998/99	20	1 try	
Adam	Kershaw	Prop	1998/99	1998/99	4		
	Krige	Wing	1998/99	1998/99	1		
Mateaki	Mafi	Wing	1998/99	1998/99	10	2 tries	Tongan
Mike	Mika	Prop	1998/99	2002/03	96	4 tries	Samoa – capped whilst at CFC(RU)
John	Munro	Flanker	1998/99	2001/02	11		
Roy	Roberts	Lock	1998/99	1998/99	1		
Richard	Saltmarsh		1998/99	1998/99	1		
Martin	Wallwork	Scrum half	1998/99	1998/99	6		
David	Warwood	Fly half	1998/99	1999/2000	2	3 points	
Nick	Watkins	Lock	1998/99	1999/2000	18	2 tries	
Kevin	Whitley	Lock	1998/99	2002/03	46	5 tries	Canada – two separate spells at Club
Simon	Amor	Fly half	1999/2000	1999/2000	11	12 points	
Matt	Aston	Lock	1999/2000	2001/01	5	1 try	
Jim	Broady	Prop	1999/2000	1999/2000	9		
Rob	Callaway	Flanker	1999/2000	2002/03	34	7 tries	3 tries v Barbarians, Warwickshire
Nigel	Cane	Scrum half	1999/2000	1999/2000	20	29 points	
Mike	Davies	Centre	1999/2000	2001/02	53	4 tries	

Players' Records

FIRST NAME	LAST NAME	POSITION	FIRST SEASON	LAST SEASON	APPEARANCES	TRIES / POINTS (if known)	REPRESENTATIVE HONOURS & NOTES
Andy	Dawling	Flanker	1999/2000	1999/2000	8		
Glenn	Delaney	Lock	1999/2000	1999/2000	29	37 points	New Zealander
Mark	Ellis	Flanker	1999/2000	2003/04	47		Two spells
Danny	Gallagher	Prop	1999/2000	2000/01	15	1 try	
Mark	Gilbert	Wing	1999/2000	1999/2000	12	1 try	
Kurt	Johnson	Wing	1999/2000	2010/11	242	99 tries	Plus 10 tries when at Rotherham
Tom	Jordan	Flanker	1999/2000	1999/2000	1		
Rob	Lowe	Wing	1999/2000	1999/2000	3		
Chris	Maisey	Wing	1999/2000	2000/01	4		Elder borther of Will
Danny	Malin	Fly half / Full back	1999/2000	2000/01	5		
Trent	McMurray	Hooker	1999/2000	2003/04	85	13 tries	New Zealander
Nick	Osman	Centre	1999/2000	1999/2000	5	1 try	
Tim	Payne	Prop	1999/2000	2000/01	26	1 try	England – not whilst at CFC(RU)
Stuart	Pearman	Prop	1999/2000	1999/2000	2		
Matt	Sims	Centre	1999/2000	2000/01	13	3 tries	
Carl	Southwell	Hooker	1999/2000	2002/03	14	2 tries	
Pete	Talbot	Centre	1999/2000	1999/2000	1		
Chris	Tarbuck	No. 8	1999/2000	1999/2000	31	4 tries	
Sam	Viggers	Centre	1999/2000	2002/03	4	1 try	
Shaun	Brady	No. 8	2000/01	2003/04	61	12 tries	
Lee	Buckby	Scrum half	2000/01	2002/03	9	1 try	
Carl	Butcher	No. 8	2000/01	2000/01	3		
Colin	Campbell		2000/01	2000/01	1		
Martyn	Davies	Full back	2000/01	2002/03	47	513 points	
Jamie	Elphick	Fly half / Full back	2000/01	2000/01	12	16 points	
Jon	Evans		2000/01	2000/01	1		
Perry	Freshwater	Hooker	2000/01	2000/01	1		
Simon	Frost	Centre	2000/01	2002/03	10	3 tries	
John	Griffiths	Lock	2000/01	2001/02	33		
James	Hayter	Hooker	2000/01	2000/01	21	2 tries	
Ian	Higgins	Wing	2000/01	2000/01	3		
Matt	Howland	Centre	2000/01	2000/01	2		

FIRST NAME	LAST NAME	POSITION	FIRST SEASON	LAST SEASON	APPEARANCES	TRIES / POINTS (if known)	REPRESENTATIVE HONOURS & NOTES
Rob	Hurrell	Lock	2000/01	2003/04	64	4 tries	Elder brother of Will
Mitch	Read	Centre	2000/01	2000/01	8		
Mark	Tinnock	Lock	2000/01	2002/03	64	14 tries	
Craig	Turvey	Scrum half	2000/01	2000/01	11		
Elisi	Vunipola	Fly half	2000/01	2001/02	49	65 points	Tonga – not whilst at CFC(RU)
Geoff	Wappett	Flanker	2000/01	2000/01	3		

Lightning Source UK Ltd.
Milton Keynes UK
UKHW021115280721
387807UK00002B/91